Dogs

Dogs

A. J. AND H. A. BARKER

Bison Books

This edition published in the USA for
K Mart Corporation
Troy, Michigan 48084

Copyright © 1983 Bison Books Corp.

Produced by Bison Books Corp.
17 Sherwood Place
Greenwich, CT 06830, USA

ISBN 0 86124 094 4

Printed in Hong Kong

PAGE 1: *Ruby Cavalier King Charles Spaniel.
The Cavalier breed originated in England
where it was crossed with other spaniels as well
as with certain toy breeds imported from
China and Japan.* PREVIOUS PAGE: *Two
Maltese. The good-natured little Maltese is
the oldest toy breed in the West. It probably
takes its name not from the island of Malta,
but from the Sicilian town of Melita. There is
evidence that this breed was established in
the Mediterranean area at the time of the
Roman Empire and was a popular pet even
then. It has changed little over the centuries.*
THIS PAGE, *left to right: German Shepherd,
German Long-haired Pointer, German Short-
haired Pointer.*

Contents

The First Dogs

For centuries, dogs have been part of the everyday life of people all over the world. Beloved by some, tolerated by others, and occasionally disliked, the dog is universally recognized as one of the most intelligent animals. Just how man and the creature which has been called his 'best friend' came to accept each other is a mystery. Originally they were enemies – rival hunters competing for similar foods – and up to the Stone Age period any kind of partnership between man and dog seems improbable. At that time the early dogs were akin to wolves, and prehistoric men and wolf-dogs were just as ready to eat each other as any other form of prey.

The domestication process took a long time, and we shall never know why or how it evolved. Perhaps the wolf-dogs prowled round man's encampments looking for opportunities to steal food or pick up a wandering child. Perhaps they were attracted by the bones and offal that men threw out of their caves, and these scraps forged a link between human and animal. In the course of the development of this relationship undoubtedly many dogs were killed. The first dogs were vicious brutes, but primitive men were equally vicious – wild creatures ready to defend their settlements against marauders with the same savagery they used in hunting. Nevertheless they had the rudimentary traits attributed to humans and, when dogs and orphaned puppies were caught, it was inevitable that some of them would be taken into the settlements. Having been reared by man, some of the puppies formed attachments with the people that fed them. Such dogs then began to identify themselves as members of the human family and their innate 'territorial' instinct led them to defend the territory of the humans that had adopted them against invaders – even their own species. With every succeeding generation of puppies born in the human settlements, the bond between man and dog grew stronger but the dogs retained their basic instincts. Primitive men feared darkness, for beyond the circle of light cast by the camp fire real and imaginary danger lurked wild animals and evil spirits, the latter no less worrying because of their immunity to attack. When it was realized that the settlement dogs were able to detect the approach of enemies long before human sentries noticed anything, they were put to work as guard dogs; through their highly developed sense of smell and hearing dogs could sense danger and raise the alarm. This enabled the men to prepare themselves for an attack. It was a short step from guarding man to guarding his other animals. As man acquired domestic animals the dog was called upon to protect them and to keep them together, that is, to act as a shepherd, and in the course of time the dog has been increasingly used in this role in the service of society.

The second basic instinct retained by the dogs born and bred in man's settlements was that of hunting. They no longer had to hunt for food, of course, since man provided that, but the natural instinct to chase and kill remained. Consequently, when early man found out that his dogs would cooperate in the hunt, they were employed in this role also and were used either to drive game in the direction of an ambush or to drag it down. Hunting in this manner went on for hundreds of years while succeeding generations of both men and dogs steadily became more and more domesticated and more familiar with each other's ways.

Undoubtedly the dog has changed considerably since the Stone Age days of the wolf-dog, and some people find it difficult to understand how so many different shapes and sizes have descended from one common ancestor. The answer is that, before today's multitude of breeds came to be recognized, a process of natural evolu-

OPPOSITE: *A Samoyed. The dog is a Spitz breed which takes its name from a Siberian tribe called the Samoyedes. It was introduced to the West considerably earlier than the other Arctic Spitz breed.*

8

tion in different parts of the world created dogs suitable for their own particular environment and conditions. This process, divergence in type, took millions of years, with mutations happening all the time. An animal which was born differing from the norm would find that this either helped or hindered him in his daily life. If the divergence was helpful, then those with the same abnormality would tend to thrive and breed in greater numbers, while those who found their mutation was a handicap would usually succumb in the struggle for survival and disappear. Thus the abnormal would become the normal until, in turn, the species took another step up on the ladder of evolution. The modern breeds of sight hound provide an excellent example of the evolution process. The original wolf-dog is believed to have been a comparatively slow animal, relying first and foremost on its sensitive nose and acute sense of hearing to find its prey, and then on its perseverence and stamina to track and eventually to catch it. On the plains and in desert country, however, speed was all important, for that was the only means of escape open to wild game pursued by its enemies. In such circumstances speed and sight were more important in the dog than the ability to detect by nose and ear. Thus a new type evolved – a rangy, long-legged, swift hunter from which are descended all the modern coursing dogs, such as the Borzoi, Greyhound, Saluki, Whippet, and Irish Wolfhound.

Primitive man would not, of course, have had any knowledge of the breeding processes inherent in the evolution of the dog. However, as the centuries rolled by, hunters and farmers would recognize that like bred like, and that a courageous dog mated to a brave bitch would usually produce puppies of a similar temperament. This would not always occur, owing to the interplay of genetical factors not understood at the time, but it was a good enough rule to ensure that breeders who required certain attributes in their dogs would stand a fair chance of success.

RIGHT: Dalmatian. The name Dalmatian implies that this breed comes from the Dalmatian coast of Yugoslavia, but various theories have been put forward that the dog originated in Denmark, Spain, Egypt or India. INSET: Dandie Dinmont. The Dandie Dinmont Terrier has a large following, especially in Britain.

Thus, by trial and error, a variety of dogs were produced – large dogs and small dogs, dogs with straight legs and dogs with crooked legs, dogs with thin coats and dogs with profuse coats – in effect, all the types of dogs which we have today.

Finally, with the passage of time, as knowledge grew, breeding became more scientific and dogs were bred for specific purposes – guard dogs, sheepdogs, hounds, pet dogs, handsome dogs, and grotesque dogs – in fact, every kind of dog for work, sport, or amusement.

Bearded Collies. All Collies come from Scotland and the name derives from an old Anglo–Saxon word Col, *meaning black. In Scotland the sheep were usually black in color and so were called 'Colleys.' The dogs that worked them were known simply as Colley Dogs. This eventually was shortened to 'Collies.'*

Dogs in the Classics and in Legend

The Greeks and Romans loved dogs and writers and teachers of both nations wrote freely in praise of them. In Greek mythology, for example, Actaeon, a huntsman, surprised the moon goddess Diana while bathing, was changed by her into a stag and torn to pieces by his own hounds.

Geryon, another character in Greek mythology, was reputed to be a monster with three heads, whose oxen ate human flesh and were guarded by Orthos, a two-headed dog. In another Greek legend, Icarius, the King of Attica, was killed by men who had drunk his wine and concluded it was poisoned. Icarius' body was buried under a tree, and his daughter Erigone was directed to the spot by the howls of his dog Maera (the glistener). Erigone promptly hanged herself from the nearest tree and Icarius, Erigone, and the faithful Maera were all carried off to the heavens and changed into constellations – becoming the Wagoner, the Virgo, and the Canis Minor.

Another of the constellations is Orion, who in mythology was a giant hunter slain by Diana and who now roams the skies attended by his dogs Arctophomus (bear killer) and Ptoophagus (the glutton of Ptoon).

The Roman Emperor Hadrian is said to have ordered a State funeral for a dog as a reward for its lifetime of fidelity. This is a virtue for which dogs have been praised since ancient times, and one of the most famous examples is that of Argus, Ulysses' dog. This dog had been parted from his master for over 20 years and was very old

OPPOSITE: Great Dane. This breed may have originated in Denmark, but there is no doubt that it was in Germany that the Great Dane reached its present standard of excellence. Its ancestors were the heavy Mastiff-type war dogs attached to Caesar's legions.

when Ulysses, disguised as a beggar, returned to his palace in Troy. An old servant who had known Ulysses since childhood failed to recognize him but in the words of the *Odyssey*:

> Near to the gates . . .
> Argus the dog his ancient master knew,
> And, not unconscious of the voice and tread,
> Lifts to the sound his ears, and rears his head,
> He knew his Lord, he knew, and strove to meet;
> In vain he strove to crawl and kiss his feet:
> Yet all he could, his tail, his ears, his eyes
> Salute his Master and confess his joys.

Dragon, a dog owned by a certain Aubry of Montdidier, earned his place in legend for a different reason. In 1371 Aubry was murdered in the forest of Bondy near Paris. Nobody saw the murder, but suspicion fell on Richard of Macaire because a snarling Dragon flew at his throat. Richard, who was ordered by the judicial authorities to fight it out with the dog, was killed, and just before he died he confessed to the crime.

King Arthur is perhaps the best-known character in British mythology and his favorite hound was Cavall. Sir Tristam, one of the knights of Arthur's Round Table, whose exploits are recorded in Malory's *Morte d'Arthur*, is said to have had a dog called Hodain or Leon.

In Celtic mythology the foremost hero-figure was a mortal endowed with super-human faculties, Cú Chulainn. His name, which meant 'Hound of Chulann,' was given to him when he was seven years old after he had been compelled to kill the

14

guard dog of Chulann the smith. But Cú Chulainn loved dogs and his favorite was called Luath – a name which Robert Burns subsequently gave to his own favorite dog and to the poor man's dog representing the peasantry in his poem *The Twa Dogs*:

> A ploughman's collie,
> A rhyming, ranting, raving billie
> Wha for his friend and comrade had
>   him,
> And in his freaks had Luath ca'd
>   him
> After some dog in Highland sang
> Was made lang syne – Lord knows
>   how lang.

Fingal, the great Gaelic semimythological hero, whose name was given to the great cavern on Staffa which is supposed to have been his home, had a dog called Bran. And the favorite of Roderick, a Spanish hero around whom many legends have been collected, was called Theron.

Then there is the legend of the Mauthe dog – a ghostly black spaniel which for many years haunted Peel Castle on the Isle of Man. It was said to go into the guardroom at dusk and, while this specter dog was there, the soldiers dare not swear or mouth obscenities. This was because a drunken trooper had on one occasion uttered a string of oaths, lost his speech and died three days later. (Sir Walter Scott refers to this dog in his *Lay of the Last Minstrel*.)

Beth Gelert, or the Grave of a Greyhound, is a ballad by William Robert Spencer, recounting an old and widespread legend which, with variations, is found in Sanskrit and other ancient literature. Briefly, the story is that a Celtic chief Llewellyn, returning home from a day's hunting, is met by his favorite hound who is covered with blood. Llewellyn runs to see if anything has happened to his baby son, finds the cradle overturned and spattered with blood. Assuming the dog had attacked the child and eaten it, Llewellyn promptly stabs the hound to death. Afterward he finds the baby quite safe, and a huge wolf under the bed, dead.

Finally there is the tale of the *Dog of the Seven Sleepers*, Katmir, who, according to Moslem tradition, was admitted to heaven. (This was a special privilege, because dogs are generally disliked by Hindus and Moslems. One exception is made with the latter; the Arabs do not like dogs except for the Saluki, which is allowed to live in the tents and is bred with great care. An Arab cannot do any man a greater honor than by presenting him with the gift of a Saluki.)

OPPOSITE: Dobermann Pinscher. The word 'pinscher' means terrier, and this dog was named after a German dogcatcher and breeder named Dobermann, who developed the breed. INSET: Dingo. This breed, native to Australia, is the only true wild breed remaining in the world.

ABOVE: These three Standard Poodles are groomed for a show. The two on the left are trimmed in the lion, or Continental clip. The one at the right is trimmed in the Dutch, or puppy clip. BELOW: Pointer. The Pointer is a gundog which searches for game.

Care and Training

Given proper attention a dog will remain healthy. The first consideration, however, is where the dog sleeps since this is a matter of paramount importance to him, is directly related to his comfort, and hence to his health. Even if he sleeps on the settee or on his master's bed, he should still have a bed or a sleeping place of his own where he can get away to snatch a quick nap. (The dog bed should be slightly bigger than the dog when it is curled up. A larger bed is not as comfortable to the dog as he likes to feel something around him while he is napping.) Dogs which are quartered outside need a snug and solid kennel which will give protection from the elements. It should be solidly constructed, however, with a windbreak at the door. Except in very cold climates, it should not be insulated. Insulation sometimes allows the humidity to build up, causing condensation to form, and this chills the dog making it susceptible to illness.

The kennel should face south (only in northern latitudes) and be slightly bigger than the dog when curled up; this permits its body heat to warm the kennel in cold weather. Finally, the kennel should be moved periodically. This not only keeps the area cleaner and allows the grass to regrow, but also helps to avoid parasite problems.

EXERCISE

A pet dog should have some sort of exercise every day. A little dog can get exercise by chasing around the garden or by just being naturally active even in an apartment. A larger dog needs to be taken for a walk or allowed to run in a fenced-off area. Dogs which have insufficient exercise are apt to become fat, develop physical defects, and may even become neurotic. Letting a dog roam at will is not a good idea; not only is it dangerous for the dog, but such practice can cause trouble for the owner as well.

OPPOSITE: American Cocker Spaniel—smaller than the British Cocker Spaniel, with a more profuse coat. BELOW: Labrador Retrievers. Some of the ancestors of this dog were Newfoundland dogs taken to Britain by Canadian fishermen who sold their catches in England.

A dog that is tied up or confined to a run should have regular periods of free exercise out of the run. Whether it is work – such as training a hunting dog or herding cattle – or just a good run in the woods, the dog will appreciate it and will not become bored. A bored dog is often a barking dog.

GENERAL CARE AND GROOMING

Care of a dog means keeping its teeth, coat, ears, eyes, and feet in good condition. Grooming is a matter of brushing and combing, clipping and stripping, shampooing and conditioning. Care and grooming go together, for if the dog is groomed regularly, many minor disorders of skin, eyes, teeth, or feet may be avoided completely, while others will be caught at an early stage when curing them is relatively simple.

The coat

The dog's coat is the dog's complexion. A rich, full, and glossy coat means that it is healthy, while a dull, dry, lifeless coat which is constantly shedding hair means that something is wrong. Normally a dog's coat sheds out twice each year, in spring and autumn, although many dogs shed a little hair all the time. Excessive shedding between the shedding seasons may occur if the dog is not well, though many pet dogs kept in a house appear to shed continually. This may be because the house is too warm and too dry for the animal. Mixing a spoonful or two of fresh fat (bacon dripping, melted lard, or finely chopped suet) into the dog's food may help to limit the shedding. Sponging the coat with a weak vinegar and water mixture should also help. (Bathing the dog will *not* help, since baths tend to dry the skin and cause itching.)

In any event all dogs need regular grooming, not only to keep their coats looking good, but to keep oil in their hair and to remove dead hair. Moreover, grooming keeps the dog comfortable. Short-haired dogs are best groomed with a stiff brush and chamois cloth. Too stiff a brush should not be used or the dog's skin may be scratched. After brushing the coat thoroughly in the direction in which the hair grows, a chamois should be rubbed a

RIGHT: Airedale Terrier. This breed is a descendant of the black and tan hunting terriers, now extinct, which were crossed with foxhounds in the Airedale Valley in Yorkshire, England. INSET: Alaskan Malamute.

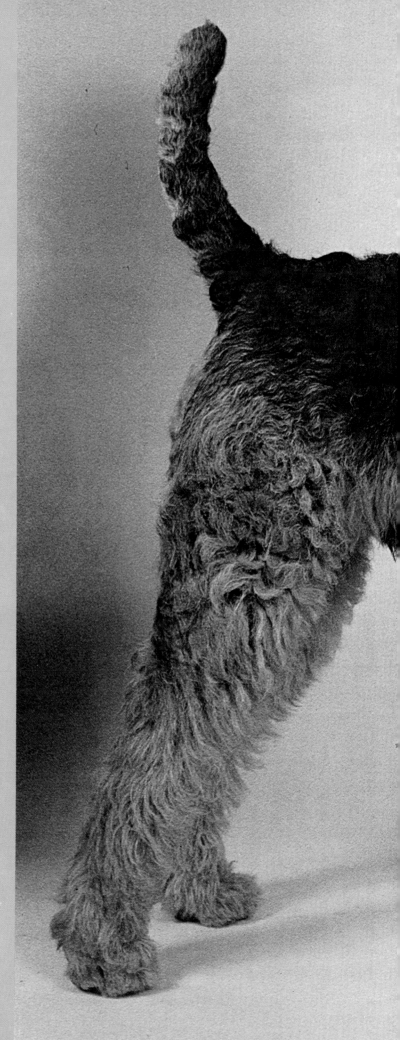

few times across it to add extra sheen to the coat. Thorough grooming of a short-haired dog, other than an occasional bath, takes only 15 minutes at most and will greatly improve the health of the dog's coat.

A medium-coated dog should be combed out first, or brushed with what is known in the United States as a 'slicker' (this is a flat brush with bent metal pins which is very effective for removing dead hair and stimulating the skin). Then the regular brush and chamois should be used.

Long-coated dogs such as Old English Sheepdogs and Afghan Hounds need more frequent grooming, first using a brush with straight metal pins, then a comb. Using a 'slicker' will tear hair out, and using the comb first will cause severe pulling if there are mats and tangles in the coat. Tangles should be eased out gently, holding the tuft close to the skin with the thumb and forefingers. Mats of tar can be removed by using an absorbent cotton pad soaked in acetone or a piece of ice. Burrs and teazles can be worked out with mineral oil, and the comb should be used only when necessary. The best tool is a brush.

The hair should be brushed every day, every single part of the head and body, legs and tail being brushed in the way the hair should lie. Thus, in the case of a smooth-haired dog, the hair should be brushed in the direction of growth to keep it trained down tight to the skin. Animals with stand-off type coats should be brushed against the grain to bring the hair up and away from the body. Long-coated breeds should always be groomed from the bottom of the legs upward to ensure that the coat

Beagle. The Beagle is a hunting dog, used to track rabbits in most countries. But they are used to hunt leopards in some countries, such as Sri Lanka and Venezuela.

is mat-free all the way through and not just on the top layer.

Finally, it is advisable to keep a careful watch while grooming for any fleas, ticks, or red, irritated areas. Taking prompt care of such problems will bring a faster cure and prevent further trouble.

The teeth

Dogs seldom have dental problems other than those caused by disease or old age. They very rarely get cavities. The main trouble is decay caused by the feeding of soft food. A soft diet, consisting mainly of canned food or table scraps, does not keep the tartar cleaned from the teeth and as this builds up, it works down into the gum, often causing infection and soreness. A few hard dog biscuits or large bones to gnaw on will often prevent this trouble, as will keeping the dog on a diet of dry dog food.

Over and above the question of maintaining the correct diet, however, periodical cleaning of the dog's teeth is advisable. A mixture of one part of cold milk to three parts peroxide is suitable, as the milk cleans the enamel and keeps the teeth white, while the peroxide eradicates any decaying particles which have worked down into the gums. Clean the teeth using swabs of absorbent cotton or a baby's toothbrush.

Tartar deposits may be scraped off with a dental scaler, pressing the scaler gently down just below the edge of the gum until it is below the tartar, then scraping it off by pressing firmly against the tooth. It will help to swab with the milk and peroxide solution afterward. Heavy tartar deposits, however, are best removed by a vet, who should also examine the dog for any foul odor or redness in the mouth.

The ears

The ears should be examined every time the dog is groomed. Not only do they frequently need cleaning – especially on long-eared dogs – but they are a favorite hiding place for ticks. Head shaking and hanging an ear down on one side are symptoms of pain, and a certain confirmation that there is trouble is an unpleasant smell coming from the ear. It is unwise for a novice to poke about in a dog's ear and, if trouble is suspected, it is best to consult a vet. Often it is just caused by the secretion of hard, brown wax, in which case a ball of absorbent cotton dipped in olive oil or liquid paraffin may be used to remove the lumps of wax. It is dangerous, however, for the inexperienced owner to use a probe in the ear, for if the dog jumps or the probing is too deep the eardrum may be punctured.

As a preventive for any form of canker in its early stages, dusting with boracic powder once a week should help to keep a dog out of trouble. But once trouble has started or been allowed to continue, then more qualified treatment is necessary.

Sometimes very tiny mites attack the ear and the dog is nearly driven mad with

BELOW: Welsh Terrier. This breed is a sort of miniature Airedale, looking something like a Fox Terrier. RIGHT: West Highland White Terrier. Scotland has five main breeds of terriers—Cairns, Dandie Dinmonts, Skyes, Scottish Terriers and West Highland Whites.

excessive irritation, and as a result is continually scratching the ear. In such cases no smell emanates from the ear.

It is absolutely essential when bathing a dog to plug his ears with absorbent cotton in order to prevent water seeping into the inner ear. So much ear trouble is caused by not taking this precaution. A single piece of cotton should be used in each ear, and if the point of the cotton to be inserted is smeared first with petroleum jelly, this will help to keep the ear even more waterproof. Needless to say, the plugs must be removed after the bath, otherwise they can work inward and cause trouble.

The eyes

The expression of the normal dog is bright and intelligent, and when he is healthy his eyes are clear and clean. A change from the normal indicates that something is wrong. A staring, dazed expression with whites showing may mean overexcitement. Watery, weeping, or heavy lidded eyes may be a sign of an infection. This is not to say that all eye troubles are necessarily serious – weeping and discharge from the eye may simply be caused by a cold, a blow on the eyeball, or weed seeds lodged under the eyelids. Inflamed, red-lidded eyes,

ABOVE: A pack of English Foxhounds— smaller and with shorter legs than the American Foxhound. LEFT: An English Setter puppy. INSET: English Setter. One of the most attractive breeds of dog, the English Setter originated from English Hunting Spaniels.

however, merit the attention of the vet.

Weeping eyes should be attended without delay. Any mucus or scaly particles should be swabbed away from the corners of the eyes with absorbent cotton soaked in water to which a small quantity of Witch Hazel has been added. Many things can cause weeping eyes – foreign particles, inverted eyelashes, blocked tear ducts being the most common – and it is as well to find out the real cause from the vet before attempting any further treatment.

The nose

To the dog the nose is more important than his eyes, although scenting ability differs with the breed. It seems to be keenest in those dogs which have a long nose, long ears, and hanging lips, such as the hounds and sporting breeds. Shape and color of the nostrils may also be important factors. The sharpest noses are generally those in which the nostrils are large, black, and open –

exceptions being the brown-nosed hunting dogs.

As the nose is also the organ of breathing, it works best when the nostrils are cool, clean, and free of mucus. (Incidentally, a cold nose as a sign of the healthy dog has been overrated.) A dry nose may be a sign of fever, although it is more often merely the result of a snooze in a warm place. A watering or mucous discharge, however, may indicate something serious. Such a discharge suggests distemper or a bronchial ailment, although it may also result from a simple cold. In any event, the nose should be cleaned with a soft cloth and the mucus in the nostrils removed with a swab; the nostrils should then be greased with petroleum jelly or olive oil to keep them soft.

The feet

Another part of the dog's anatomy which needs regular and careful inspection is the feet. In many breeds, the hair between the pads on the underneath of the foot must be removed. This should be snipped away with a pair of small scissors; great care must be taken because it is easy to snip the pad. It is best to wash the feet first, soaking the pads and working between them with the fingers. This will remove any clots of dirt and, when the foot is dry, facilitate the snipping out of the hair.

Pads should also be regularly inspected for thorns, cuts, and cracks. Tiny stones will lodge between the pads, causing soreness if they are not noticed and removed at once. Tar is another problem, and often small lumps get embedded in the crevices of the pads when dogs are taken on tarred roads in very hot weather. They are difficult to remove and often a combination of soaking and cutting out is necessary.

Occasionally a dog may spend a lot of time biting and nibbling his feet, and the base of the nails will be seen to be in a slightly crusted, sore condition. In this case the vet should be consulted because the condition is usually caused by a fungus, rather similar to athlete's foot.

The dog's nails should be checked periodically. In most breeds nails are kept naturally short by exercise on hard surfaces and therefore need no cutting. Many house dogs, however, fail to wear

RIGHT: Basenji. This dog cannot bark, merely yodel. INSET: Basset Hound. The Basset was used originally in France and Belgium for hunting deer, rabbits and hares. Later it was crossed with the Bloodhound.

down their nails naturally and they can grow so long that they spiral until they stick into the pad. Such a condition is very painful and can lead to permanent damage if not quickly taken care of. The normal, well-worn-down nail is about even with the bottom pads of the foot, so that when the dog walks the nails just brush the ground. Nails should have a blunt appearance. When they begin to develop a hook, they are too long. A nail trimmer is a handy and inexpensive purchase and, with a little practice, almost anyone can keep their dog's nails trimmed and neat. When beginning, only a little bit should be taken from each nail. There is a vein that runs down the nail, and if the nail is clipped too short, it will bleed. Should this occur, a dab with a styptic pencil or a pinch of finely ground potassium permanganate crystals will quickly stem the bleeding.

Special care for the aged dog

Older dogs often need special care to live out their lives in the best possible health. To begin with, the old dog cannot walk as fast or as far as he used to, so his exercise should be restricted; short walks at a more leisurely pace should be the order of the day, so that he does not get overtired. He will also want to sleep more, and should be allowed to do so – in a softer bed, warmer in winter, cooler in summer, because he feels the cold and the heat more in old age.

Teeth should be carefully watched as they wear down. Older dogs are often fed canned foods which do not remove the deposits of tartar that accumulate on the remaining teeth. These tartar deposits work into the gums, causing sore and inflamed gums, and then infection sets in. The teeth loosen and the dog is unable to eat at all.

The mouth should be checked periodically for irritation or redness. If there is any foul odor or sign of loose teeth, the dog should be taken to the vet for treatment before the condition becomes worse. All tartar accumulations should be removed as they form and not be allowed to build up to thick, irritating scales.

Deafness, which is quite usual in aged dogs, need not curb his activity but it may risk his safety. The first sign may be apparent inattention or disregard of words of command. The dog is not actually being disobedient – it is just that he cannot hear. To call him it will be necessary to tap on the ground to attract his attention or, if his eyesight is still good, to wave to him.

BELOW: Bloodhounds. The Bloodhound's ancestors were French, although now it is considered to be a British breed.
RIGHT: Border Terrier. INSET: Border Collie. Both of these breeds originated in the Cheviot Hills in the border country of Scotland.

Blindness is more serious than deafness in the old dog. As his sight fails he may well show signs of fear because he cannot see clearly. Not moving the furniture around and keeping things such as his bed, water bowl, and so on, in the usual places will ease his problems. This is even more important if he loses his sight completely. A dog which is totally blind can get around quite well and still enjoy life if a little extra care is taken.

AILMENTS AND ACCIDENTS

Abscesses

Abscesses are the result of a local infection and may appear on any part of the body. If possible they should be treated daily with a hot poultice. Ready-made poultices such as kaolin may be used; alternatively liquid garlic or witch-hazel should be heated and seaweed powder added to make a paste, which should be spread on lint. This should be applied to the affected part, and then covered with gauze and bandaged. The treatment should be continued until all the discharge has come away. If the abscess is in a difficult position where it is not feasible to apply a poultice, it should be treated with hot fomentations of salt water (one tablespoonful of salt to one cup of water). The dog's diet should also be watched and garlic tablets given three times a day.

Anal glands

A dog has two small glands, one on either side of the rectum, called anal glands. These are scent glands and they empty into the rectum during a bowel movement or at times of fright. Unfortunately, the opening into the rectum sometimes becomes plugged with fecal material and does not allow the gland to empty. Thus the gland fills and can become infected. A dog with a full anal gland will drag its rear end on the ground or carpet in an attempt to squeeze this accumulation out of the gland. People used to think this meant the dog had worms, but this is not so. Worming a dog with infected anal glands can be dangerous, for constipation often goes along with the condition and, if the dog cannot get rid of the wormer, it may make it sick or even kill it. A vet can show you where the anal glands are and how to empty them yourself. If the glands are checked and emptied if necessary, they will not be so prone to infection. Feeding a diet of dry dog food or giving several hard dog biscuits daily will often help prevent the condition, as

RIGHT: English Springer Spaniel, one of the eight different varieties of spaniel dogs.
INSET: English Toy Terrier.

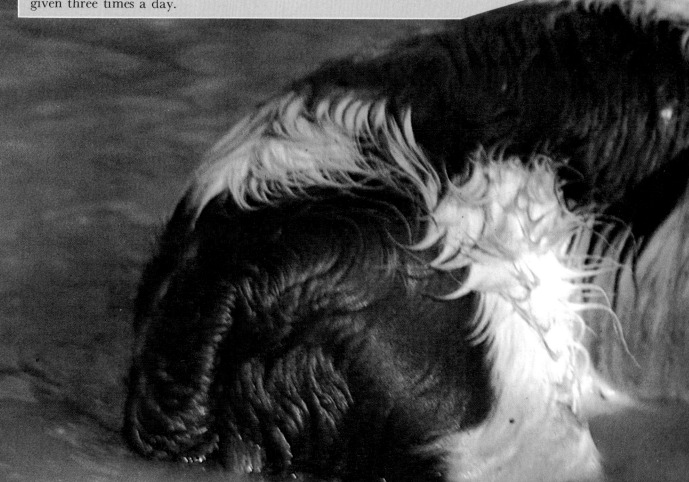

soft stools cannot empty the glands. Feeding a diet that will give a firm stool will aid the dog in emptying the glands naturally. Exercise will usually help too. In any event a dog should have the anal glands checked at least twice a year, smaller dogs about twice a month, since plugged anal glands can result in abscesses, lameness, and even hindquarter paralysis.

Anemia
This is manifested by lack of pigmentation, that is, a pale nose. It is a dietary condition caused by lack of iron and can be rectified with a course of elderberry tablets.

Appetite
If a dog is suffering from a lack of appetite, providing he is otherwise in good health he will regain his appetite if given a gastric mixture or gastric tablet before his meal and one wheatgerm capsule twice a day.

Arthritis
Arthritis is often a problem with older dogs, especially with heavy, obese dogs. It is important that the old dog not be allowed to get fat. There is a tendency toward stiffness in old age, and the extra weight only intensifies the problem, making it crippling in many cases. Treatment with drugs, such as cortisone, aspirin, phenylbutazone, and chlorphensin carbamate,

will often help dogs with periodic pain. Keeping the dog warm, in dry quarters, and off cement will aid in prevention of stiffness.

Often confused with arthritis, in older dogs especially, is lameness due to long or ingrown toenails. With less exercise, older dogs' nails do not wear down normally and require periodic trimming. If this is not done, the nails will grow, curl, twist, and even grow into the pad of the toe. This causes terrific pain, and the dog will be reluctant to move about; when it does so, it will limp badly. (see 'The Feet,' p. 234).

Bad breath
This may be the result of incorrect feeding – especially tidbits. Clean the dog's mouth and teeth and give him daily garlic pills.

Bites, cuts, and abrasions
Dogs suffer from the same kind of injuries as humans, including cuts, bruises, and scrapes; bites are more usually associated

ABOVE: Borzoi. The Borzoi came to the West from the USSR, and until recently, was known as the Russian Wolfhound. It has a friendly temperament. RIGHT: Boston Terrier. During the nineteenth century Bulldogs were crossed with Terriers to produce the Boston Terrier, which was used in the cruel sport of dogfighting. It is a dog that is easy to train.

with the animal world. However, the same type of first aid used for humans is indicated for these forms of dog injury. If the wound is minor it should be cleaned with liquid garlic or salt and water and then painted with iodine. However, if the cut or bite is a deep one, the bleeding may be stopped by putting a pad over the wound and applying pressure to stop the flow of blood until the vet's advice can be sought.

Broken bones or fractures

All too often these are a result of automobile accidents. When a dog has been struck by a vehicle the first two things to be feared are shock and internal bleeding. A broken leg or gash are minor worries when compared to these. Lift the dog gently on to a blanket or rug. On no account grab the animal around the waist or chest as this can push a broken rib through a lung.

Do not try to give the dog any food or water; an injured dog is usually in shock and is in no condition to take either.

Severe vomiting can result, which could start internal bleeding. Take the dog immediately to the vet. Often an injection of a clotting drug, stimulant, or immediate surgery can save the dog that would die otherwise.

Bruises

A bruise is bleeding under the skin and dogs sometimes get bruises just as humans do. However, a dog's skin is looser, allowing more bleeding, and the bruises fill with blood making a lump called a hematoma. They are often found on ears, due to flapping the ears in attempts to get rid of itching ear mites or dirt accumulation.

FAR RIGHT, ABOVE: Standard Schnauzers. BELOW: Giant Schnauzers. RIGHT: Miniature Schnauzer. The name of these dogs comes from schnauze, German for snout or muzzle. The two smaller varieties are Germany's equivalent of the British terrier breeds. The forebears of the Giant Schnauzer were sheepdogs and cattledogs in South Bavaria that were mixed with other breeds.

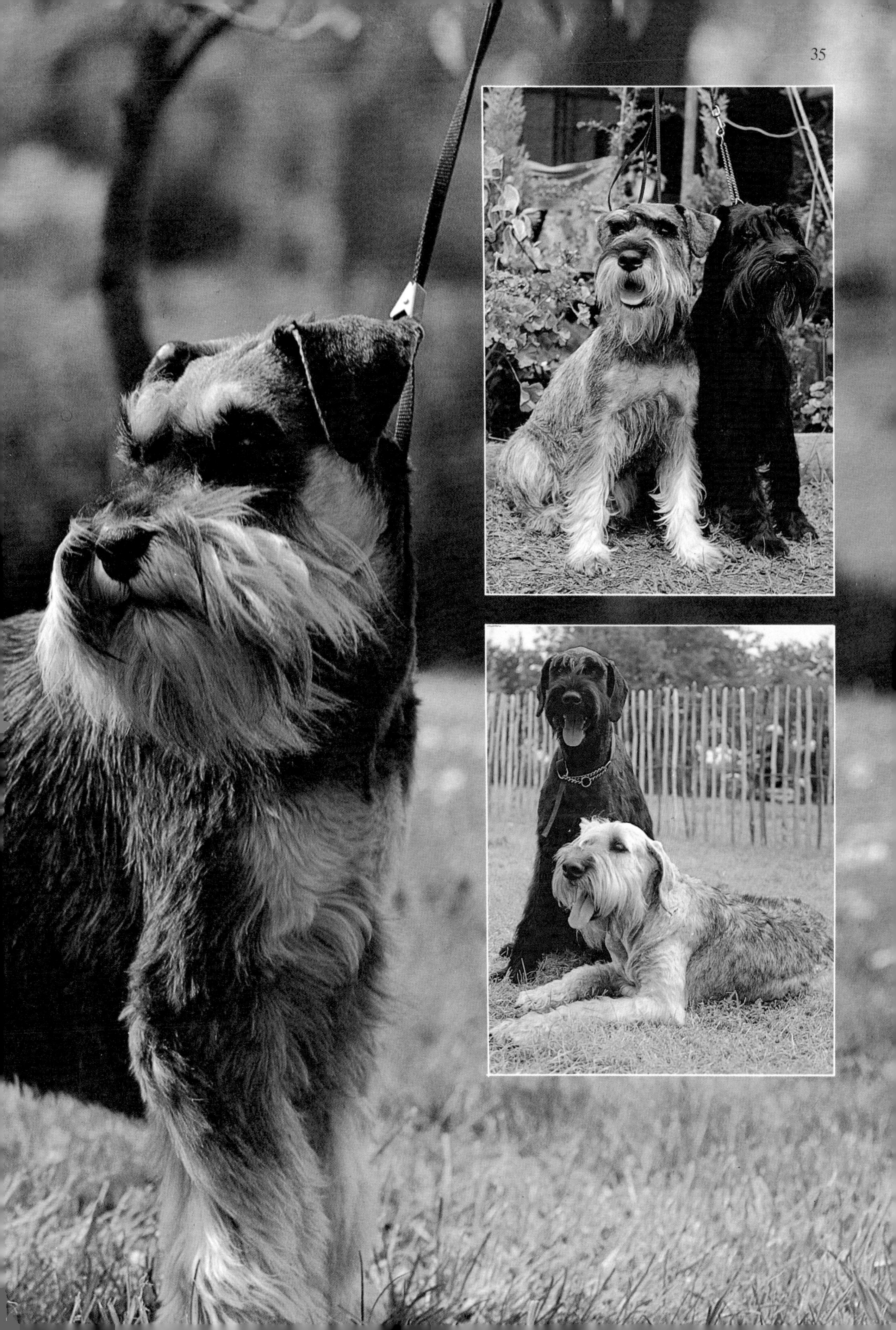

They are also often found on the neck from collar injuries, such as occur when a dog on a chain lunges forward. Bruises should be treated by a veterinarian.

Burns and scalds

Needless to say, every effort should be made to avoid dogs acquiring burns or scalds in the first place. All fires should be well guarded and all hot cooking pans kept out of reach. Should the dog become burned or scalded, however, the affected parts should be dressed with an antiburn or boracic ointment, covered with absorbent cotton, and bandaged up. Subsequently the burn/scald should be dressed twice a day with ointment until it is healed. If the burn/scald is a sizable one, the vet should be consulted and the animal kept quiet as it will probably be suffering from shock.

Coat

A dull coat, a thin coat, or 'staring' (lacking in body or sheen) may be a sign that the dog is out of condition or even that he has worms. If the coat is molting or thin, its condition may be improved by augmenting his diet with raw, red meat. Meantime a thorough daily grooming is essential.

Constipation

A dog that is being fed incorrectly or not getting sufficient exercise may become constipated. Cure by dosing with castor oil or olive oil until the bowels recover. Plenty of exercise is very necessary.

Cystitis

Cystitis is an inflammation of the bladder. It is quite common in dogs, but not always diagnosed, as many times there is just a mild inflammation which causes no visible problems. Cystitis is most frequently caused by bacterial infections and stones (calculi).

A dog with cystitis often urinates frequently, vomits, dribbles urine unconsciously, and appears to be restless. Lifting up the dog may bring yelps of pain. Often there is blood in the urine. Where the cystitis is caused by a stone, there may be a complete blockage of the urethra and the dog is not able to urinate. Consequently it absorbs the wastes, becomes toxic, and within a short time the dog is in serious trouble.

With an infection in the bladder, medication usually brings prompt relief, but the infection must be correctly diagnosed. Surgery is the best treatment for a dog with stones, as they are usually quite large and nearly impossible to dissolve.

Diabetes

Diabetes is a disease that strikes dogs as well as people, and it most often occurs in fat dogs over four years of age. The first signs are an increased thirst and frequent urination, then there is a weight loss, quickly getting to the point of emaciation. In severe cases there is uncontrollable vomiting. When caught fairly early, and when there are no complicating factors, diabetes can be controlled quite easily if the owner is willing to spend a little extra time with the dog daily. As with humans, mild cases may be controlled by diet alone; the carbohydrate intake is severely cut, and the dog is fed foods such as lean meat, boiled eggs, and boiled fish. Other cases respond well to oral medication. Still other dogs need insulin injections daily, given before meals. The needle used is very small, and the injection is practically painless.

Diarrhea

Diarrhea is nature's way of ridding the body of impurities and no attempt should be made to stop it unless it persists. The dog should then be fasted for 24 hours on honey and cold boiled water; it should also be given a mild laxative pill. Feeding should then commence with a white-meat diet.

If the diarrhea is persistent it could be a warning sign of more serious trouble – possibly coccidiosis, a disease caused by the parasite *Coccidia*. (Coccidiosis most often affects puppies, although adult dogs are often carriers and can affect young dogs. Damp, unsanitary conditions, and overcrowding help to spread the disease.) Dealing with this type of infection is beyond the capability of the normal dog owner and the vet should be called in.

Distemper

Sometimes called the 'canine plague' because of its widespread occurrence and virulence, distemper is one of the most

OPPOSITE: Old English Sheepdog. Sometimes called the 'Bobtail,' this breed is about 200 years old. It was originally a working dog used to protect herds of cattle from beasts of prey, but it has recently become more commonly a pet and companion.

serious of all the diseases of dogs. The virus causing distemper is airborne and can affect dogs of any age, although it is most serious in puppies under a year old because such young dogs often do not have the strength to combat the disease.

The most common symptoms of distemper are: discharges from the nose and eyes; diarrhea and vomiting; an offensive odor from the skin, caused by slight skin eruptions; sneezing and coughing; loss of appetite; and sensitivity to light. Should an owner suspect his or her dog has distemper, the dog must not come into contact with other dogs, and the owner should avoid visiting other people with dogs since the disease is highly contagious. This is one instance where the vet should visit the owner – on no account should the dog be taken into a waiting room full of dogs. Treatment, once the disease has got under way, is often frustrating for both the owner and the vet. The sick dog may look better and show signs of recovery one day, but then get worse the next. Antibiotics will not cure the disease, as it is a virus, but they can prevent secondary infections such as pneumonia.

Ear infections, Ear canker

Dogs, especially long-eared dogs, are prone to several types of ear infection. The most common is ear mites, which burrow into the ear, creating places for bacteria and fungi to enter. The moist, dirty ear that often accompanies the mites makes a perfect breeding place for these infections, and such bacterial and fungal infections cause considerable trouble. They often get a start from irritation due to dirt and wax accumulation, water or shampoo in the ear, foreign bodies, or injuries.

An infection can be suspected if the dog constantly scratches its ears with its hind feet, and rubs its head on the floor or against a chair. The dog may also shake its head, hold it to one side, and appear in pain. The inside of the ear is often red and swollen, may have a brownish, foul-smelling accumulation inside, and be hot.

Mild cases, caused by accumulation of wax and· dirt, may be taken care of at home. An absorbent cotton swab should be dipped into methylated spirits and the ear swabbed out. The treatment should be repeated for two days. There should be a great improvement, but if not, the dog should be taken to the vet, for a severe canker is a task for him alone. Ear mites

are so tiny that they cannot be seen by the naked eye.

Eclampsia

The most common form of this is the drying up of a bitch's milk. More often than not it is a small bitch with a fairly large litter that is affected. She will begin to pant, stumble, and fall when she attempts to walk and she may have convulsions. If not treated she will die.

The puppies should be taken from the bitch and handreared, and the bitch taken to the vet who will give her an intravenous injection of calcium. Most bitches respond rapidly, but they must be fed on plenty of raw, red meat.

Eczema

In hot weather it is quite common for dogs to start scratching, biting, and licking themselves. Sometimes the remedy is to change to a white-meat diet; in any event the dog should get plenty of exercise. When the eczema progresses it causes bald patches, especially at the base of the tail and on the front feet. Irritation can be eased by swabbing the affected parts with methylated spirits or washing with a light disinfectant soap and then applying a skin balm. All the dog's drinking water should be boiled.

Epilepsy, fits, and hysteria

Epilepsy is quite often seen in dogs, especially in some of the smaller breeds; Miniature and Toy Poodles and Cocker Spaniels are quite often affected. This is not to say many of these dogs have epilepsy, but only that it is more common in them than in Alsatians or Great Danes.

A dog with epilepsy will have recurrent 'fits' or convulsions. The dog shakes, stiffens out, falls, and jerks its legs; its head often tips backward. Excitement may trigger these seizures. They may occur only once a year or several times daily, and they do not last long. If the dog is running around, catch it and put it in a quiet and cool, darkened room. Then apply cold water compresses to the head. If the seizure persists, the vet should be

Finnish Spitz. This dog (Suomenpystykorva in Finland) is virtually unknown outside of that country. But in Finland it is the most popular breed. It is kept both as a pet and as a hunter.

called in, for if epilepsy is diagnosed he can prescribe oral drugs which will usually keep the dog from having further seizures.

Eyes

Inflamed and 'weeping' eyes should be treated immediately. The eyes should be bathed very gently with absorbent cotton swabs dipped in boric acid or sodium bicarbonate solution to remove any dirt or pus. A simple eye ointment like mercuric oxide should then be applied. Castor oil and cod-liver oil are old-fashioned eye soothers, and a drop of one or the other should be placed in each eye before the dog is taken out for a run in woods and fields. They help insure against the scratching and discomfort caused by dust, pollen, and weed seeds. Proprietary eye preparations for humans are excellent for dogs. There are also modern eye ointments which the veterinary may prescribe.

Inverted eyelids and in-growing eyelashes sometimes occur. These cause continual weeping and pawing of the eye and the vet should be called in.

Fleas

When dog parasites are mentioned most people immediately think of fleas. In fact, fleas are a problem with very few dogs as long as a few preventive measures are taken.

Fleas are tiny, fast-moving, flat insects which suck blood and annoy dogs and people. Dog fleas will bite humans! Sandy, dry areas are favorite spots for fleas. They do not spend their life on the dog, but hop off and on. This is why, when treating the dog with a flea spray or powder, its bedding, rug, or sleeping place must also be treated.

If the dog does collect some fleas, groom it daily and apply an antiparasite powder, making sure it gets right down to the skin. Brush out one hour after applying. Bedding, baskets, and kennels should also be treated by dusting the powder well into the fiber or cracks in the woodwork. For an effective dip, see Ticks.

Fungus infections

Fungus infections are often mistaken for mange by the layman. However, there are many types of fungus infections that can attack dogs, the most common producing bald, angry, red spots which appear either to itch intensely or to be very tender. Such spots usually occur on the neck and back and spread outward. The hair must be clipped from around the spot and the area treated with an antifungal ointment prescribed by the vet.

Heart trouble

Old dogs, like old people, often develop heart trouble; overweight dogs are especially prone to it. Often the first signs that heart trouble is present are coughing and enlargement of the abdomen. A dog with heart trouble will often have poor circulation, with fluid settling out of the blood and into the tissue. This can often be controlled by use of diuretics, which stimulate the kidneys, drawing fluid out of the body. Salt intake should be restricted. There are also oral drugs, given to strengthen the heart, but these must be prescribed by the vet who will also advise on the dog's diet.

Hepatitis

Hepatitis is caused by a virus and is therefore easily spread, often by the urine of infected dogs. Its symptoms resemble those of distemper. There is usually a fever, inflamed eyes, vomiting, no appetite, and diarrhea. The dog may develop white eyes, which can cause temporary blindness. This usually follows the acute period of the disease, where the dog is sickest; if it is not treated, it will usually disappear in a week or two. This condition is called 'blue eye.' The same condition sometimes sets in with distemper, continual weeping, or injury. It usually clears without treatment. However, the only safe means of prevention of hepatitis is to vaccinate susceptible dogs.

Lice

Lice are tiny, slow-moving, grayish parasites which occasionally infect dogs. They do not move about like fleas but hook into the skin, hold fast, and suck blood. They are most often seen on medium-coated or long-coated breeds, as the long hair enables them to hide from the light. When lice are bothering a dog, the dog will usually begin to scratch excessively. On parting the hair it is possible to see the tiny lice and the little specks which are their eggs.

When lice are discovered on a dog, the entire dog should be clipped short. With

OPPOSITE: Newfoundland. One authority has claimed that the Newfoundland is descended from Pyrenean Mountain Dogs (Great Pyrenees) taken to Newfoundland in the middle of the 17th century.

no hair to hide in and protect them from an insecticide, the lice are usually easily taken care of. There should be a repeat treatment every week for three weeks to kill any new lice that have hatched out. The dog's bedding should be burned and its bed dusted with the same powder or spray as is used on the dog.

Mange

Mange is quite common in dogs in some parts of the world. It is transmitted by tiny mites which cannot be seen with the naked eye (and which are often carried by humans on their skin!). The mange mites burrow into the dog's skin causing intense itching. Malnutrition accompanied by poor skin health often gives mites a start. Skin eruptions, especially about the face, legs, and belly, should be regarded as suspicious.

Pustules, scabby areas, thickened, grayis areas, and baldness are all symptoms mange.

Mange is very contagious to othe animals, so a dog suspected of having mange infection should be isolated until has been seen by a vet. Treatment entai completely clipping the dog and the use medicated shampoos and special ointmen which only the vet can prescribe.

Obesity

Obesity is often due to incorrect feedin coupled with too little exercise and to many tidbits. A normal, balanced diet wit a day's fast once a week and plenty exercise should cure the condition in tim

Rabies

Rabies is an infectious disease affectin many warm-blooded animals, includin

an. (It used to be termed 'hydrophobia' cause paralysis of the throat made it fficult for a rabid animal to drink.) It is ore common in dogs than in any other imal, but it can affect and be trans-itted by rodents, cattle, horses, cats, onkeys, and other animals.

There are two types of rabies: dumb bies, in which the dog just sits, mouth ten hanging open, and has a peculiar ok in its eye, and furious rabies, when a g has hallucinations, snaps at imaginary bjects, is restless and irritable. Often, the mb rabies is the more dangerous, as any people pry into the mouth, thinking e dog has something in its throat or outh. Getting the dog's saliva into a nall cut or scratch can give you rabies, never try it. Not all rabid dogs, however, tack people and have frothy mouths. A

rabid dog often has a personality change. A timid, fearful dog will become brave and friendly; a normally friendly dog will turn surly and timid. A rabid dog will often leave home and wander until exhausted.

There is no treatment for rabies once symptoms have developed in dog or man. Vaccination will provide protection, however.

LEFT TO RIGHT: Miniature Bull Terrier, Bull Terrier, Cairn Terrier. The Bull Terrier was developed by the British for use in dogfighting. Bulldogs were crossed with Terriers. Other crosses were then made which gave the Bull Terrier its characteristic conformation and its more controllable temper. The Miniature Bull Terrier is merely a small-sized Bull Terrier. The Cairn Terrier was developed in Inverness, Scotland and is basically a pet.

Snake bites

A snake bite requires immediate first aid. Where the fangs have punctured the dog's skin the wound should be opened – with a knife, a nail-file, or similar instrument – and potassium permanganate crystals or damp Epsom salt should be sprinkled in. If there is a rapid swelling apply a tourniquet between the bite and the heart, loosening for a few seconds every few minutes. *Get the dog to a vet as soon as possible, for time is important.* (Most snakes are not venomous but the bites of nonvenomous ones can turn poisonous and so, for safety's sake, the punctures should be inspected and cleaned by a vet.)

Stings

For a bee sting apply baking soda; for a wasp sting, liquid garlic; for a hornet sting apply alternatively a hot, then cold poultice of liquid garlic.

Ticks

Ticks are blood-sucking parasites which dogs that roam woods and fields – especially near cattle – are apt to pick up. There are several types of ticks but all are basically the same.

In small numbers they generally cause no trouble except irritation. In large numbers, however, they can produce anemia and extreme agitation. Scratching and biting at the tick bites breaks off the tick heads, irritates the skin, and aggravates the dog's problem. Secondary infections often follow, and generally ticks can get into the ear canal, causing ear infections and irritation.

Ticks may be removed simply by pulling slowly but firmly. If they are yanked off, the mouth may be left behind to cause infection and soreness. Spots that look sore should be wiped with methylated spirits or iodine. Dips should be used regularly in tick-ridden areas, and flea-powder will also help. (An effective dip to kill ticks on the dog may be made with 4 oz of derris powder containing 3 to 5 percent of rotenone and 1 oz of flaked soap in a gallon of tepid water. For the dip the dog's eyes should be protected by applying petroleum jelly or oil around them. The same wash with half the amount of derris can be used for fleas.)

Travel sickness

All foods should be withheld before a journey.

Tumors

Breast tumors are sometimes seen on aged, unspayed bitches. They may or may not be malignant. With some tumors, injections of testosterone will result in regression of the growths. Spaying the female will also help in some cases. Surgery is recommended for dogs in good health, while the tumors are still small in size; if they are allowed to grow large, the chances of successful surgery are greatly reduced. Thus as soon as lumps on the breast are detected, they should be looked at by a vet.

Worms

Several types of internal parasites – worms – may be harbored by dogs. They can be inherited but more commonly the worm larva is taken into the dog's organs through its food. The most common are roundworms, tapeworms, hookworms, whipworms, and headworms. (The latter is most common in the south of the United States and is usually fatal.)

Worms can sometimes be detected in the dog's excrement, but a microscopic examination is usually necessary to determine the type of worms present. External indication of the presence of worms include excessive appetite, laziness, loss of weight, eye excretions, and vomiting. These symptoms are common to other dog ailments, however, and therefore are not positive guides; only a microscopic investigation of the dog's stool can ascertain whether or not worms are present. Treatment for worms varies according to the types present and should not be undertaken without the advice of a vet.

TRAINING

Training may be said to start with the education of the puppy, whose first lessons will necessarily be simple ones. To start with he needs to know his name and respond to it when called. The name itself should be short and crisp and pronounced clearly in a moderate tone of voice whenever the puppy is called. It will not take him long to connect his name with himself, especially if he is praised when he responds.

The next lesson is concerned with the

RIGHT: Pekinese. It is estimated that this breed has been in existence for some 2000 years, having been developed as a miniature dog in China. In 1860, when the Summer Palace in Peking was sacked by the French and British, five dogs were taken to England.

collar and leash. The puppy must first be familiarized with the wearing of a collar and, when he has learned to accept it, a lightweight leash or piece of string should be attached. The puppy should then be allowed to wander around, trailing the leash quite freely until he is familiar with that too. Then the real lesson starts. The owner should pick up the end of the leash and guide the puppy around the room. At first he may well resent the slight tugs at his neck which the guiding process entails, but he will soon come to disregard the tugging and accept that he is expected to go where his master leads him. As with all training, patience and understanding are the key factors.

Simplest of the puppy's early obedience lessons is persuading him to go to his bed. This merely entails him learning to understand that when he receives the command 'Bed' or 'Basket,' he is expected to go to his sleeping place. The association of the command with his bed can be strengthened by dropping one of his toys into the bed when the order is given. Eventually he will come to understand what is wanted but the owner may have to be persistent, as well as patient – and lavish with praise when the puppy shows signs of confusion.

In talking to a dog a friendly, conversational tone – not too loud and not too soft – should be used. A sharp, quick manner of speaking may be used for correction, while soft, slower tones are used for teaching. Address him clearly and distinctly, using as few words as possible and the same commands each time (for example, if 'Bed' is the order for him to retire, it should not be alternated with 'Basket'). Talk to the animal as you would to a child of limited understanding. When you say 'Ball' to a child and show him a ball, he learns to connect the sound with the object. A dog will do the same, and if this is kept up with a variety of objects, a dog will sometimes become so smart that certain words which you do not want him to latch on to may have to be spelled out.

Training a dog to 'Sit' and 'Stay' are important early lessons. Both commands are intended to curb the dog's activity, and 'Stay' is merely an extension of 'Sit.' The latter is taught during leash training and accomplished by a sharp pull on the leash and, if need be, by firmly pressing down his hindquarters until the dog assumes a sitting position. The 'Stay' exercise follows when the 'Sit' lesson has been learned. With the leash in the owner's left hand and the dog on the left, the right hand, palm flat, is brought up in front of the animal's face and he is told in a firm voice to 'Stay.' If he moves, the leash is given a short, sharp jerk to make him sit, and the command 'Stay' is repeated. The exercise is performed for only a few seconds at a time to begin with, then for longer, with the owner moving away and the leash going slack. If the dog gets up to follow, he should be taken back to the same spot and the lesson repeated. This exercise should be repeated with the dog standing up and lying down until the dog obeys the command every time.

For a dog to come when called is clearly important; if he is not taught to do so the dog will come when called only when he wants to, and one day he will refuse and perhaps end up under a truck. The lesson is best taught after the 'Sit-Stay' exercise has been mastered. A long length of cord should be attached to the collar and the dog ordered to 'Stay.' The owner then walks away from the dog to the end of the cord. Facing the pupil the owner then orders 'Come.' If the dog does not start forward, the owner can try slapping his knee as an added invitation. If he still refuses, a light tug on the cord should get him moving.

The 'Come-when-called' exercise should be practiced day after day until the dog responds to the command promptly, no matter how far he is let out on the cord. Later he should be tried off the leash in an area where he cannot run out into traffic. If he continues ignoring the command 'Come,' the owner should turn round and walk away. A dog that merely wants his master to play will be disappointed, change his mind, and return. If he does so, the owner should again be lavish with his praise. On no account should the dog be called to its master for disciplining; if the dog is to be scolded the owner should always go to the animal.

Training a dog to be clean about the house – house-training – generally starts when the puppy is between three and six months old (the actual age depends on

OPPOSITE: Lhasa Apso. This dog is sometimes called the Tibetan Apso. It is a true Tibetan dog, and the Dalai Lama himself often presented them to high-ranking foreign visitors. Apso is the Tibetan word for goat.

the size, type, and intelligence of the individual dog). The earlier one starts on the training, the more the pupil requires to relieve himself, and thus the teacher has to be ready to take the dog out more often. Everything, in fact, depends on how careful and alert the teacher is. House-training is a full-time job; a puppy simply cannot be trained in the morning and not in the afternoon, or trained for a few days and then left for a day or so. The object is to teach the dog to adapt to man's way of life. He is by nature a clean animal and with patience he will respond to the training very quickly.

By the time the training starts the puppy's master should have a reasonable idea of his dog's needs. At four or five months of age a puppy urinates and empties his bowel quite often. Cold, excitement, and confusion add to the number of times he needs to go and feeding almost always promotes the urge. This means that he will have to be taken outside the first thing in the morning and thereafter at two-hourly intervals. It is a good idea to watch the puppy's behavior just before he relieves himself; when he is about to urinate he rushes around sniffing the floor or the ground before squatting, and when about to defecate he generally turns round and round on a particular spot. These are sure indications and, as soon as he is seen to embark on these preliminaries in the house, it is best to pick him up, carry him out, and set him down to complete his business.

When the puppy is taken out he should be set down on the ground and, when he has relieved himself, he should be praised and petted and then taken in again. After his breakfast he should be taken out again. It is a good idea every time he is taken out to say 'Want to go out? Go out?' until the puppy associates the words 'Go out' with the need to relieve himself. And when he is taken out he should remain outside until

RIGHT: French Bulldog. It is described as a miniature version of the British Bulldog. In 19th century Paris the French Bulldog became a sign of fashion. FAR RIGHT: Bouvier de Flanders. The Bouvier came from Belgium where it was used for herding cattle.

something has been done. There will be mistakes, of course, until the animal learns to control his bladder and bowels; when he does make a mistake he must be corrected immediately. Correction should be limited to scolding, *never* a spanking, as the latter will merely frighten him. Puppies which are spanked while being house-trained will inevitably continue to make mistakes.

Traffic

Like humans, dogs have to come to terms with the automobile. To ensure that a dog does not constitute a menace to itself or to others on the road, it must be either kept on a leash, or so well brought up and disciplined as to behave well at all times. (Many people do not appreciate that, if a dog causes an accident, its owner is held to be responsible for the damage, and this can be an expensive business.) The trouble is that roads and automobiles are alien to his nature and, although it is possible to train dogs to cope with traffic, very few are. In any event, according to a study conducted by a Viennese vet who observed the behavior in traffic of 400 dogs, very few canines are fit to run off the leash. Those that did behave well were police dogs and guides for blind people – big dogs which had had a long, specialized, and intensive training.

LEFT ABOVE: Long-haired Dachshund. LEFT BELOW: Wire-haired Dachshund. ABOVE: Smooth-haired Dachshund. Dachshund in German means 'Badger Dog,' and is one of the most popular breeds. There are six varieties: standard and miniature sizes in Long-haired, Smooth-haired and Wire-haired.

The dog in the automobile

Today's dog travels a lot in an automobile, and for some canines there is no greater pleasure than being driven around. Other dogs cannot tolerate automobiles. They become sick and nervous, wanting to be out of the vehicle and generally making the journey miserable for the other passengers. In the majority of cases the answer to this problem is training. This should be initiated when the dog is a puppy. Short drives will get him used to the motion of the vehicle, and giving him no food or water for at least two hours before a journey should help him to overcome automobile sickness. A passenger holding him on his or her lap, or sitting him on the seat beside him/her, will help to give him confidence. Letting the dog see out of the window also helps and discourages sickness, but he should not be allowed to lean out of the window as the rush of air may cause cold in his eyes and ears.

On no account should the dog be forced into the automobile while he is being taught to accept it. If he is afraid he should be put into the vehicle for a short time while it is stationary; gradually he will become accustomed to it and can be taken for a short drive. If, during the period of trial runs, the dog becomes uneasy, it is best to stop and let him out of the vehicle, taking him for a short walk before driving him home again. Most dogs gradually become used to the idea and become travel enthusiasts. For those who are less enthusiastic and who get excited and sick, the vet can prescribe drugs which have a soporific effect.

The trunk is no place to carry a dog; he will be confined in a dark, restricted space, and during the journey he may swallow dust, lethal exhaust gases, and gasoline fumes. As the trunks of most cars are located close to the rear axle, the wretched animal will also feel every bump in the road.

Leaving a dog in a parked automobile in the sun with the windows closed is equally as callous as transporting it in the trunk. If the dog has to be left in the automobile, the vehicle should be parked in the shade with the windows lowered a few inches on either side. If he has been kept on a leash, this should be removed to ensure he does not strangle himself, and, if the owner is to be gone any length of time, a bowl of water should always be left on the floor.

It is perhaps unnecessary to remind the reader that, if one takes a dog on a long journey, he must be given an opportunity to run around three or four times a day and to perform his natural functions. (Needless to say, special care has to be taken if the dog exercises near a busy road.) Finally, a light diet is recommended for a long journey: dog biscuits and canned food are probably the most convenient form, and plenty of water should be made available when the meal is given – especially in hot weather.

Dogs and television

For humans television is now an established facet of modern life, and in the United States the dog-food industry has financed television programs for dogs. Their value is debatable but it can be argued that big business rarely sinks money into publicity ventures which will not show any return.

For many years a specific point was made that dogs cannot recognize moving pictures. However, an American scientist has claimed to have proved that dogs' mouths actually watered when the animals under test were shown a film of other dogs being fed. In all probability the reason for this was that the appearance of the dogs on the screen was combined with barking and yelping—noises to which any normal dog will react. So far as television is concerned, dogs may be classified either as 'curious,' who become addicts, or 'uninterested,' to whom the small screen holds no attraction.

Travelling with dogs

Travelling with a dog inevitably creates problems. In recent years hotels have become more disposed toward dogs but, before undertaking a journey which includes a stay at a hotel, it is advisable to determine whether dogs are welcome.

As a general rule the smarter (and more expensive) the hotel, the more likely it is to accept dogs on the grounds that the guest is king and kings are expected to have an entourage. However, the entourage is expected to behave with decorum, and to take consideration of other guests. Thus a dog can only be left on his own in a hotel room if, in the absence of his owner, he does not bark or howl – or vent his feelings on the furniture.

Some hotels will supply dog food, but it is as well to remember that nothing is more detrimental to the dog's digestive system than strongly spiced hotel leftovers. The charges for accommodating dogs are usually based on size and whether or not food is provided.

Before one gets to the hotel, however, there is the journey. Travel by automobile has already been covered; the alternatives are the railroad and airplane. By train the dog usually travels in the guard's van in many countries, and he has generally to be accommodated in a closed (and ventilated) box which has been clearly labelled with the name and address of the owner, and the animal's destination. Before the journey it is desirable to let the dog sleep a couple of nights in this box in order to get him used to the idea of being cooped up; in the box he should have his own familiar blanket.

In an airplane the dog travels in the air-conditioned section of the plane's hold, in a special dog box with water and food. At stops en route the owner can not normally see his pet, but on long journeys overseas the ground staff – who are responsible for seeing the dog is comfortable and exercised – are often happy to relax this rule. It is perhaps unnecessary to mention that there are special rules governing the movement of animals from one country to another. Britain, for example, requires an imported dog to spend six months in quarantine, and the minimum requirements elsewhere are certificates of good health and vaccination.

RIGHT: Long-coat Chihuahua. FAR RIGHT: Smooth-coat Chihuahua. These are the two types of this dog that is named after the Mexican state and city of Chihuahua. The Smooth-coat, however, may be the true Mexican breed.

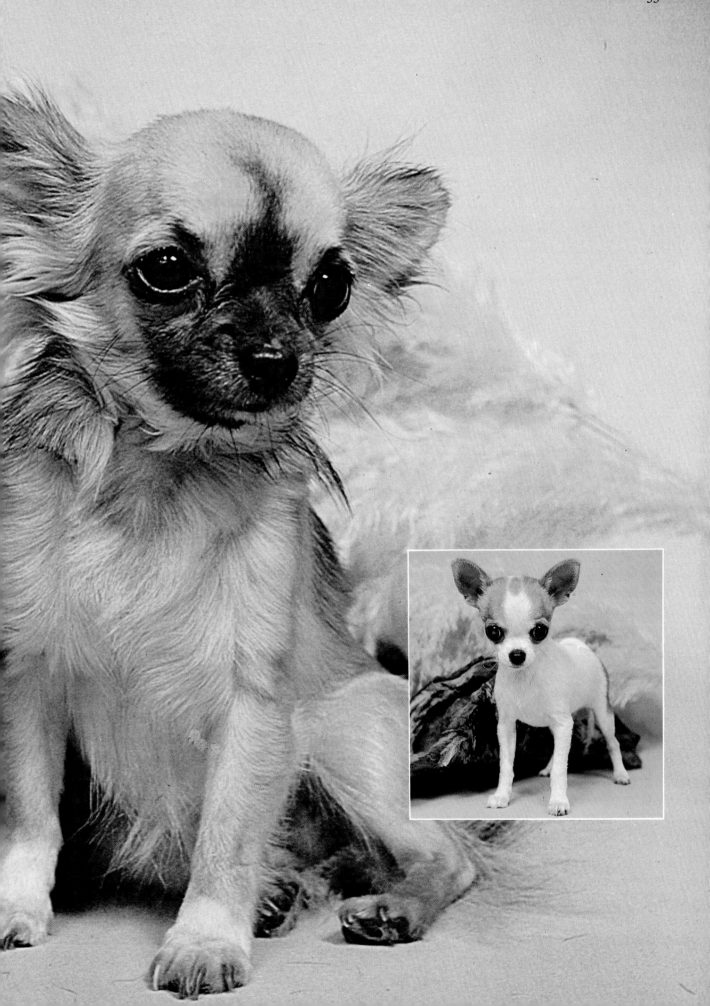

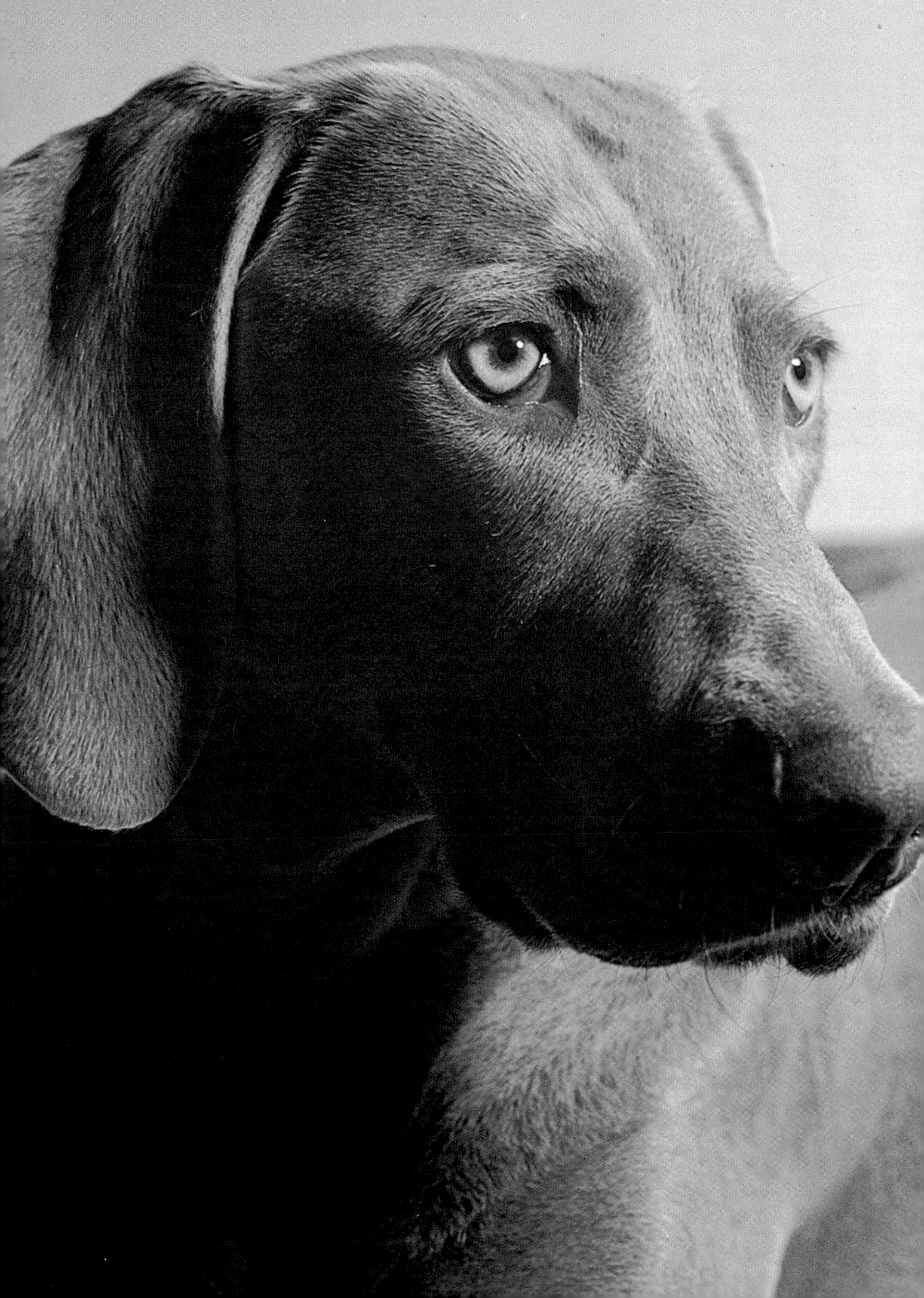

Fat dogs and fat people

As a footnote to this chapter comes a recommendation that owners who have fat dogs should watch their own weight. United States' vets say that obesity is a major health problem for America's millions of pet dogs. By one estimate, 28 percent of the domestic dog population a decade ago were overweight. More recently it has been estimated that 30 to 60 percent of all pet dogs are obese, with the health of 20 percent of those in imminent danger. The main reason: mismanagement by pet owners.

America's 45 million dogs and 25 million cats can do little about the quality or quantity of food they eat. Many dogs will eat relatively unpalatable things simply as part of a social interaction with their masters. And obesity overloads the various systems of the animal, creating much more work for the heart. Dogs in the wild travelled in packs and lived in a feast or famine situation. As a result they have a survival instinct that involves a sense of not knowing where their next meal is coming from. Boredom can also be a factor. In any event the studies in the United States indicate that overweight dogs tend to be owned by overweight people. Americans spent $2000 million on pet foods in 1978, nearly three times the $725 million spent in 1969, according to the Pet Food Institute, a trade association. To stay healthy, dogs must be properly fed, as much harm and illness is caused by incorrect feeding, not only the type of food but when and how it is given. In their natural surroundings in the wild, dogs would hunt and kill their prey and eat its raw flesh, including the intestines, stomach contents, and bones. They would drink from streams and ponds and seek out wild fruits and grasses with which to satisfy their nutritional needs and balance their diet. The modern, 'civilized' dog cannot do this; he is wholly dependent on his master/mistress and, although a mature dog can live on a wide variety of diets, many of these will not keep him in the best of health; a poor diet may even shorten his life by several years. A growing puppy is even less able to stand a poor diet.

A correct diet is based on the natural foods which dogs would seek out if they lived the way nature intended. Protein is the most important nutrient. However, if the diet is to be correctly balanced, a certain amount of vitamins and minerals must also be present as well as sufficient carbohydrates and fats. Protein is needed for body growth and maintenance. It gives energy and is also frequently combined with fatty acids; these fatty acids are needed for a good skin and coat. Carbohydrates mostly produce energy, and fiber is also needed for efficient digestion. Of the minerals that are needed for good health, it is sufficient to mention calcium and

BELOW: Field Spaniel. The Field Spaniel shares the ancestry of the other Spaniel breeds, but has remained a working breed and is normally seen at field trials rather than at formal dog shows.

LEFT: The Weimaraner has an excellent nose and is useful for both tracking and retrieving.

phosphorus which are required for the teeth and bones; iron, copper, and cobalt are needed for healthy red blood cells.

Translating these requirements into practical terms, it follows that – as with humans – fresh food is best. The main constituent of the dog's meal should be meat. This should be fed raw, for if it is cooked it loses a lot of its goodness and the food is broken down so that the dog's teeth and its digestive system have little work to do, with the result that the latter deteriorates. (For this reason no minced, soft, or sloppy foods should normally be included in the diet.)

Good dog meat is expensive and fortunately there are a number of alternatives to lean, red meat. Ox cheek, heart, and raw tripe all have good nutritional value, and fish can be substituted for meat one or two days a week. Liver is also a meat but it should be given only once or twice a week. Offal, such as heart, lights or kidney, can be given occasionally but they should be cooked. White meats, such as chicken or rabbit, are useful alternatives in corrective diets, that is, when the dog is unwell. Raw meat should be given in large chunks, and all the bones should be removed from chicken or rabbit; fish should have the bones taken out after cooking.

A certain amount of green vegetables must supplement the meat. These should be chopped small and fed raw. Parsley and watercress are best since these contain iron and vitamins A and C. Other suitable vegetables are spinach and cabbage; root vegetables other than carrots are not suitable. Carrots, however, are good for dogs – either grated into the meat dish or given to the animal to gnaw. 'Roughage' is also an essential part of the diet, and lack of roughage is responsible for a lot of anal gland trouble. In a natural raw diet roughage can consist of wholemeal biscuits, or wholemeal bread baked or toasted and cut into biscuit-sized pieces.

Contrary to popular belief that they bring sheen to a dog's coat, eggs are not especially good for dogs. The only time they really are beneficial is when an animal needs extra protein, that is, after an illness or for a stud dog. The yolks of eggs may be fed raw, but uncooked white of egg destroys an important vitamin, biotin, in the intestines. Whole eggs generally should be cooked.

The majority of dogs like bones and in many cases bones are good for the animals –

RIGHT AND BELOW: Bulldogs. In the 14th century these dogs were used in the cruel sport of bullbaiting. They were trained to seize the bull by the nose and not to let go until the bull fell and the fight ended. BOTTOM: Bullmastiff. The heavy and powerful Bullmastiff is believed to be the result of crossbreeding Bulldogs with Mastiffs. They are used as guard dogs.

Course objectives

These overall course objectives will give you an idea about what to expect from the course. It is also possible that they will help you see that this course is not the right one for you. If you think you either lack the prerequisite knowledge or already know most of the subject matter to be covered, you should let your instructor know that you think you are misplaced in the class.

Note: In addition to the general objectives listed below, specific Microsoft Office Specialist exam objectives are listed at the beginning of each topic. For a complete mapping of exam objectives to Course ILT content, see Appendix A.

After completing this course, you'll know how to:

- Create and format sections in a document, create multiple columns, and sort text in columns.

- Work with tables by formatting the cell text, resizing rows and columns, adding borders and shading, using the Table AutoFormat command, and drawing a table.

- Import Excel data into Word tables, use formulas to perform calculations, and link and embed Excel data.

- Create and modify styles to format text and to set up and use different views, including Outline view, the Document Map pane, and thumbnails.

- Create specialized headers and footers for the first page, odd and even pages, and sections, and use the page numbering feature.

- Print single labels and envelopes.

- Add graphics and objects by inserting files, Clip Art, WordArt, symbols, and drawn objects, and change the document appearance by using background colors and fill effects, watermarks, and themes.

- Use and create templates, view and edit document properties, modify template fields, and protect templates.

- Manage document revisions by tracking changes while editing, using the Compare and Merge features, working with comments, and saving different versions of a document.

Skills inventory

Use the following form to gauge your skill level entering the class. For each skill listed, rate your familiarity from 1 to 5, with five being the most familiar. *This is not a test.* Rather, it is intended to provide you with an idea of where you're starting from at the beginning of class. If you're wholly unfamiliar with all the skills, you might not be ready for the class. If you think you already understand all of the skills, you might need to move on to the next course in the series. In either case, you should let your instructor know as soon as possible.

Skill	1	2	3	4	5
Inserting section breaks					
Formatting sections					
Formatting text into columns					
Inserting and deleting column breaks					
Adding text and headings to columns					
Sorting text in a column					
Merging cells					
Changing text orientation and row height					
Distributing columns evenly across a table					
Adding borders and shading to cells					
Setting the default table format					
Importing data from an Excel worksheet					
Formatting data in a table					
Creating and modifying a chart					
Creating formulas to perform calculations on table data					
Embedding Excel data in Word					
Linking Excel data in Word					
Creating and applying styles					
Creating a document outline					
Using the Document Map pane and thumbnails					
Creating odd and even headers and footers					

Skill	1	2	3	4	5
Creating section headers and footers					
Formatting page numbers					
Adding page numbers with chapter numbers					
Printing single labels and envelopes					
Inserting graphic files and Clip Art					
Inserting WordArt					
Adding background colors and fill effects					
Adding watermarks					
Applying themes					
Using the drawing canvas and drawing tools					
Inserting a conceptual diagram					
Using a template to create a document					
Creating and protecting templates					
Viewing and editing document properties					
Creating a custom template					
Adding and modifying template fields					
Applying formatting restrictions					
Tracking changes while editing					
Reviewing revision marks and changes					
Restricting edits to tracked changes					
Merging revisions					
Inserting comments					
Printing comments					
Comparing document versions					

Topic C: Re-keying the course

If you have the proper hardware and software, you can re-key this course after class. This section explains what you'll need in order to do so, and how to do it.

Computer requirements

To re-key this course, your personal computer must have:

- A keyboard and a mouse
- Pentium 233 MHz processor (or higher)
- 128 MB RAM
- 1 GB of available hard drive space
- CD-ROM drive
- SVGA monitor (800×600 minimum resolution support)
- A printer driver (An actual printer is not required, but you will not be able to complete the printing activities in Units 6 and 9 unless a driver is installed.)
- An active Internet connection

Setup instructions to re-key the course

Before you re-key the course, you will need to perform the following steps.

1 Install Microsoft Windows 2000 Professional on an NTFS partition according to the software manufacturer's instructions. Then, install the latest critical updates and service packs from www.windowsupdate.com. (You can also use Windows XP Professional, although the screen shots in this course were taken using Windows 2000, so your screens might look somewhat different.)

2 Adjust your computer's display properties as follows:

   a Open the Control Panel and double-click Display to open the Display Properties dialog box.

   b On the Settings tab, change the Colors setting to True Color (24 bit) and the Screen area to 800 by 600 pixels.

   c On the Appearance tab, set the Scheme to Windows Classic.

   d Click OK. If you are prompted to accept the new settings, click OK and click Yes. Then, if necessary, close the Display Properties dialog box.

3 Connect to the Internet. The course assumes that your computer is connected to the Internet, so some screens and activities might look different if your computer is not connected.

4 Install Microsoft Office 2003 according to the software manufacturer's instructions, as follows:

   a When prompted for the CD Key, enter the 25-character code included with your software.

   b Select the Custom installation option and click Next.

   c Clear the check boxes for PowerPoint, Outlook, Publisher, and Access.

   d Select "Choose advanced customization of applications" and click Next.

   e Next to Microsoft Excel for Windows, click the drop-down arrow and choose Run all from My Computer.

   f Next to Microsoft Word for Windows, click the drop-down arrow and choose Run all from My Computer.

   g Next to Office Shared Features, click the drop-down arrow and choose Run all from My Computer.

   h Next to Office Tools, click the drop-down arrow and choose Run all from My Computer.

   i Click Next, and then click Install to start the installation.

5 If necessary, install a printer driver. If a printer was connected to the computer during the installation of Windows, there will be a driver installed for that printer. If not, you should install a standard PostScript printer driver, such as the HP Laser Jet 5.

6 Start Word and reset any default settings that you might have changed (or perform a fresh installation of Word according to the preceding instructions). If you don't want to change your custom settings, some activities might not key properly. Settings that need to be reset include:

- Reset list numbering to the default settings:

   a Choose Format, Bullets and Numbering.

   b Activate the Numbered tab.

   c Select each format box and click Reset (if this button becomes available).

   d Click OK.

- In the Clip Art task pane, clear the Search for box and click Go.

- Delete My note.dot, My agenda.dot, and My employee.dot from the Templates folder for Office 2003. In Windows 2000, the default path for this folder is C:\Documents and Settings\<user_name>\Application Data\ Microsoft\Templates, where <user_name> represents the current user.

- Reset the Track Changes options to match Exhibit 9-2 in Unit 9. To do so:

   a Choose Tools, Track Changes.

   b On the Track Changes toolbar, click Show and choose Options.

   c Reset the options as shown in the exhibit, and then click OK.

- Reset the Compare and Merge settings. To do so, choose Tools, Compare and Merge Documents, and then clear Legal blackline.

- Dock the Formatting toolbar below the Standard toolbar.

- Hide the Language bar.

When you're done, close Word.

7   If necessary, download the Student Data files for the course. (If you don't have an Internet connection, you can ask your instructor for a copy of the data files on a disk.)

   a   Connect to www.courseilt.com/instructor_tools.html.

   b   Click the link for Microsoft Word 2003 to display a page of course listings, and then click the link for Word 2003: Intermediate, Second Edition.

   c   Click the link for downloading the data files, and follow the instructions that appear on your screen.

8   Copy the data files to the Student Data folder.

CertBlaster test preparation for Microsoft Office Specialist certification

If you are interested in attaining certification, you can download CertBlaster test preparation software for Word 2003 from the Course ILT Web site. Here's what you do:

1   Go to www.courseilt.com/certblaster.

2   Click the link for Word 2003.

3   Save the .EXE file to a folder on your hard drive. (**Note**: If you skip this step, the CertBlaster software will not install correctly.)

4   Click Start and choose Run.

5   Click Browse and then navigate to the folder that contains the .EXE file.

6   Select the .EXE file and click Open.

7   Click OK and follow the on-screen instructions. When prompted for the password, enter **c_word**.

Unit 1

Working with sections and columns

Unit time: 40 minutes

Complete this unit, and you'll know how to:

A Create and format sections in a document.

B Format text into multiple columns.

C Enter and sort text in columns.

Topic A: Creating and formatting sections

This topic covers the following Microsoft Office Specialist exam objective.

#	Objective
WW03S-3-5	Inserting and deleting breaks (This objective is also covered in Topic B, as well as in *Word 2003: Basic*, in the unit titled "Controlling page layout.")

Section breaks

Explanation

You might want to format parts of a document differently. For example, you might want certain pages to contain several columns, and other pages to have one. You can do this by dividing the document into sections.

A *section* is a portion of a document in which you can set certain formatting options, such as line numbering, number of columns, headers or footers, and page orientation. By default, a document has only one section. You can have several sections within a single page and apply different formats to each one.

Inserting section breaks

To divide a document into sections, you need to insert section breaks. The four types of section breaks are Next page, Continuous, Even page, and Odd page. Section breaks are visible only if the Show/Hide ¶ button is selected. To insert a section break:

1   Place the insertion point where you want to insert the section break.
2   Choose Insert, Break to open the Break dialog box, as shown in Exhibit 1-1.
3   Under Section break types, select the desired type.
4   Click OK.

The following table describes the four types of section breaks:

Type	Description
Next page	Starts a new section on the next page.
Continuous	Starts a new section on the same page.
Even page	Starts a new section on the next even-numbered page.
Odd page	Starts a new section on the next odd-numbered page.

Exhibit 1-1: The Break dialog box

Deleting section breaks

To delete a section break, place the insertion point just before the break and press the Delete key.

Do it!

A-1: Inserting section breaks

Here's how	Here's why
1 Start Word	Click Start, and choose Programs, Microsoft Office, Microsoft Office Word 2003.
2 Open Responsibilities	(From the current unit folder.) You'll divide this document into sections.
Save the document as **My responsibilities**	In the current unit folder.
3 Scroll through the document	It contains a title and three major groups of information: the executive summary, project team information, and the company's plans.
4 Click ¶	(The Show/Hide ¶ button is on the Standard toolbar.) To view nonprinting characters.
5 On page 1, place the insertion point as shown	Outlander·Spices¶ Roles·and·Responsibilities¶
6 Choose **Insert**, **Break...**	To open the Break dialog box.
Under Section break types, select **Continuous**	With this setting, the new section will begin on the same page.
Click **OK**	To insert the section break.
Observe the status bar	Page 1 Sec 2 1/2
	(In the lower-left corner of the window.) It displays the current section number, 2.
7 Place the insertion point as shown	·well·as·a·justification·for·the·project. |The·project·team¶ ntly·made·up·of·six·employees·and·fo
	(Scroll down, if necessary.) You'll insert another type of section break here.
8 Open the Break dialog box	Choose Insert, Break.
Under Section break types, select **Next page**	With this setting, the new section will begin on the next page.
Click **OK**	To insert the section break and close the Break dialog box. The project team content is now on page 2, section 3.
9 Update the document	

Section formatting

Explanation

You can apply different types of formatting to different sections. You can change the orientation of a section to Landscape and apply different page margins and borders to each section. To change the page layout for a section:

1　Choose File, Page Setup to open the Page Setup dialog box.

2　From the Apply to list, select This section.

3　Specify the desired settings, and then click OK.

Do it!

A-2:   Formatting sections

Here's how	Here's why
1　Place the insertion point in page 2	If necessary.
2　Choose **File, Page Setup...**	To open the Page Setup dialog box. The Margins tab is activated by default.
Under Orientation, select **Landscape**	To change the section's page orientation.
3　Click the **Layout** tab	To view the various layout options.
Click **Borders**	(The Borders button is in the lower-left area of the Page Setup dialog box.) To open the Borders and Shading dialog box. The Page Border tab is activated.
4　Under Preview, click the indicated button	
	To apply a left border to the section.

5 Under Preview, click the indicated button

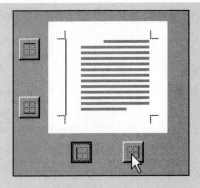

To apply a right border to the section.

6 From the Apply to list, select **This section**

To apply the borders to the selected section.

7 Click **OK**

To close the dialog box and apply borders to the section.

8 Preview the document

(Choose File, Print Preview.) The pages appear in landscape orientation and have left and right borders.

Press ⌈ PAGE UP ⌉

The first page of the document has a portrait orientation and no borders. This page is not part of the section that contains the project team details.

Click **Close**

(The Close button is on the Print Preview toolbar.) To close the Preview window.

9 Update the document

Topic B: Working with multiple columns

This topic covers the following Microsoft Office Specialist exam objectives.

#	Objective
WW03S-3-3	Applying and formatting columns (This objective is also covered in Topic C.)
WW03S-3-5	Inserting and deleting breaks (This objective is also covered in Topic A, as well as in *Word 2003: Basic*, in the unit titled "Controlling page layout.")

Formatting text into columns

Explanation

When creating documents such as brochures or reports, you might want to organize the information in multiple columns. When you create multiple columns, the first column is filled first and the other columns are filled as you enter more information. The content moves to the first column of the next page only when all columns on the current page are filled.

You cannot view multiple columns in Normal view because it displays information in a single-column format. You must switch to Print Layout view to see the multiple columns.

To format existing text into multiple columns:

1   Select the text (or section) to be arranged in columns.
2   Choose Format, Columns to open the Columns dialog box, as shown in Exhibit 1-2.
3   Under Presets, select a format. If you need more than three columns, enter the value in the Number of columns box.
4   Adjust the width and spacing of the columns as required. (As you change the various settings in this dialog box, observe the Preview area to get an idea of how the selected text looks.)
5   Click OK.

You can also format text into columns by using the Columns button on the Standard toolbar. When you do so, however, you are limited to a maximum of four columns, and you can't specify the column width or spacing. Of course, you can change these settings later by using the Columns dialog box.

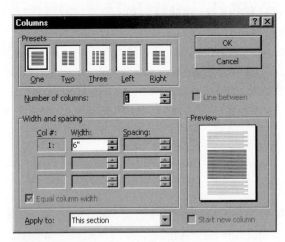

Exhibit 1-2: The Columns dialog box

The following table describes some of the options in the Columns dialog box:

Option	Description
Number of columns	Specifies the number of columns.
Width	Specifies the width of each column (in inches).
Spacing	Specifies the amount of space between columns (in inches). This setting applies to the space to the right of the selected column.
Equal column width	Creates columns of equal width.
Apply to	Specifies the part of the document to which you want to apply the column formatting.
Start new column	Moves the text after the insertion point to the beginning of the next column.
Line between	Adds a vertical line between columns.

Do it!   **B-1:   Formatting text into columns**

Here's how	Here's why
1 Place the insertion point anywhere in page 2	(If necessary.) You will arrange the project team text in columns.
2 Choose **Format**, **Columns...**	To open the Columns dialog box.
3 Under Presets, select **Two**	To format the text into two columns.
4 Check **Line between**	To add a vertical line between the two columns.
Click **OK**	To apply the specified formatting.
5 Observe the pages	Only pages 2 and 3 are divided into two columns.
6 Update the document	

Inserting column breaks

Explanation

A *column break* is a mark that indicates the end of a column. When one of the columns is longer than the other, you can insert a column break to make them the same size. The text following the break will move to the next column. You might also want to start a paragraph at the beginning of a column to improve readability.

To insert a column break:

1 Place the insertion point where you want to insert the column break.
2 Open the Break dialog box.
3 Under Break types, select Column break.
4 Click OK.

Adjusting the spacing between columns

You can adjust the spacing between columns to provide balance in a document. For example, if the columns are too close together, the text might be difficult to read. If the white space is too great, the column text might appear to be falling off the page. To adjust the spacing:

1 Select the columns between which you want to adjust the spacing.
2 Choose Format, Columns to open the Columns dialog box.
3 Under Width and spacing, in the Spacing box, enter the measurement (in inches).
4 Click OK.

Do it!

B-2: Inserting column breaks and defining the spacing

Here's how	Here's why
1 On page 2, place the insertion point as shown	party¶ 12/6/05 → Attend·a·meeting·with·the·accou **Jack·Thomas,·VP·Sales¶** Jack's·role·is·to·ensure·that·the·sites·we·choos
	You'll insert a column break so that "Jack Thomas, VP Sales" (and the text that follows it) is moved to the beginning of the next column.
2 Open the Break dialog box Select **Column break**	Break types ○ Page break ◉ Column break ○ Text wrapping break
Click **OK**	To insert the column break, which appears at the end of the first column. The next paragraph shifts to the beginning of the second column. In addition, the column text flows onto the next page.

3 Place the insertion point as shown

> as the project spokesperson for the pre
> **Ron·Timmons,·Senior·Buyer¶**
> Ron's·role·is·to·ensure·that·the·spices·
> for·the·markets·we·are·entering.·He·wi

You'll insert a column break here so that "Ron Timmons, Senior Buyer" shifts to the beginning of the next column.

4 Insert a column break

Open the Break dialog box, select Column break, and click OK.

5 Insert a column break before "Kathy Sinclair"

To move "Kathy Sinclair" to the beginning of the next column.

Insert a column break before "Thomas Boorman"

6 Observe the spacing between the columns

You'll decrease the spacing between the columns.

7 Open the Columns dialog box

Choose Format, Columns.

Edit the Spacing box to read **0.4"**

To reduce the spacing between the two columns.

8 Verify that the Apply to box reads **This section**

Click **OK**

The space between the columns has decreased.

9 Update the document

Adding a heading across columns

Explanation   You might want to give a common heading to all the columns to identify them and separate them from other parts of the document. To add a new heading across columns:

1   Place the insertion point where you want the heading to appear.
2   Type the text.
3   Press Enter.
4   Select the text.
5   Click the Columns button on the Standard toolbar, and select the 1 Column format.

The text will span both columns and will be followed by a continuous section break.

Do it!   ### B-3:   Adding a heading across columns

Here's how	Here's why
1 Select as shown	**The·project·team**¶ ·team·is·currently·made·up·of·six· You'll make this text the heading for both columns.
2 Click	(The Columns button is on the Standard toolbar.) To display the Columns list.
3 Select the indicated option	 1 Column To make the text "The project team" span both columns.
Deselect the text	A continuous section break is inserted after the heading.
4 On page 2, place the insertion point as shown	 The·project·team¶ ·and·four· Jack·Thomas,·VP· des·the· Jack's·role·is·to
Press (↵ ENTER)	To add some space between the heading and the columns.
5 Update the document	

Deleting column breaks

You can delete column breaks the same way you delete section breaks.

To delete a column break, place the insertion point just before the break, and press the Delete key. You can also double-click the column break to select it, and then press Delete. When the column break is deleted, the text shifts to the previous column.

B-4:   Deleting a column break

Here's how	Here's why
1 On page 3, place the insertion point as shown	**Kim·Leong,·Customer·Service·Representative¶** Kim's·role·is·to·oversee·the·support·of·new·and·c will·monitor·the·demands·on·our·current·system· specify·upgrades·to·our·telephone·system.·Kim·w integral·role·in·determining·the·requirements·of·a system,·and·he·will·oversee·the·creation·of·a·trair documentation·for·the·new·system.¶ ·····················Column·Break··········
2 Press ⌷ DELETE ⌷	To delete the column break. "Kathy Sinclair" now follows "Kim Leong."
3 Update the document	

Removing columns from a document

If you want a multiple-column document to be one column, you can remove the extra columns. To remove columns from a document:

1 Select the columns or the section containing the columns.
2 Open the Columns dialog box.
3 Under Presets, select One.
4 Click OK.

You can also remove columns by clicking the Columns button on the Standard toolbar and selecting 1 Column.

B-5: Removing columns

Here's how	Here's why
1 Insert a Next page section break before "Our plans"	To move the "Our plans" paragraph to the next page.
2 On page 4, select the "Our plans" paragraph as shown	
	To change the formatting back to one column, which is the default setting.
3 Display the Columns list	Click the Columns button on the Standard toolbar.
From the list, select **1 Column**	To apply the default layout.
Deselect the text	The page contains only one column. The landscape orientation and left and right borders that you applied remain.
4 Update the document	

Topic C: **Working with text in columns**

This topic covers the following Microsoft Office Specialist exam objectives.

#	Objective
WW03S-3-3	Applying and formatting columns (This objective is also covered in Topic B.)
WW03E-2-1	Sorting content in lists and tables by specific categories

Adding text and headings

Explanation

You can add, edit, and delete text in columns just as you would with the text in a one-column layout. You can also sort data arranged in columns.

You can add text to columns by placing the insertion point in the desired position and typing the text. As you add text to a column, the length of the column increases to accommodate the new text. If the end of the column is reached, text wraps to a new column. You can also add headings by typing text and then applying the necessary formatting.

Do it!

C-1: Adding text and headings to columns

Here's how	Here's why
1 On page 2, place the insertion point at the beginning of the first column	¶ The·Expansion·Project·team· outside·consultants.·This·mix You'll insert a column heading here.
2 Type **Introduction** Press (↵ ENTER)	
3 Apply **Arial**, **Bold** formatting to the new heading	¶ **Introduction**¶ The·Expansion·Project·team·is
Deselect the text	If necessary.
4 In Ann Salinski's information, place the insertion point as shown	Her·schedule·for·the·coming·week:¶ 12/3/05 → Attend·a·session·on·the·upcoming· 12/1/05 → Review·the·estimated·expenditure· 12/6/05 → Attend·a·meeting·with·the·account
5 Type **12/2/05** Press (TAB)	
6 Type **Hold a meeting with the team to discuss party expenditures** Press (↵ ENTER)	Her·schedule·for·the·coming·week:¶ 12/2/05 → Hold·a·meeting·with·the·team·to·discuss·party·expenditures¶ 12/3/05 → Attend·a·session·on·the·upcoming·financial·report·¶ 12/1/05 → Review·the·estimated·expenditures·for·the·Christmas·party¶ 12/6/05 → Attend·a·meeting·with·the·account·executives¶
7 Update the document	

Sorting text in columns

Explanation

After you've entered text in columns, you can sort it by number, text, or date in ascending or descending order. When a column contains text, *ascending* means alphabetical order (A-Z), and *descending* means reverse alphabetical order (Z-A).

To sort text in a column:

1 In the column, select the text that you want to sort.
2 Choose Table, Sort to open the Sort Text dialog box, shown in Exhibit 1-3.
3 Under Sort by, from the Type list, select the item by which you'll sort the text.
4 Select either Ascending or Descending.
5 Click OK.

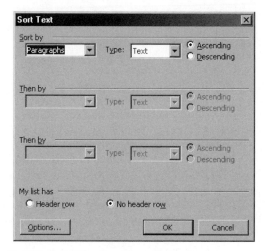

Exhibit 1-3: The Sort Text dialog box

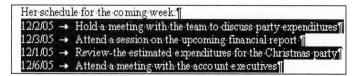

Exhibit 1-4: The selected schedule for Step 1

C-2: Sorting text in a column

Here's how	Here's why
1 Select Ann Salinski's schedule	(As shown in Exhibit 1-4.) The dates are in a random order. You'll sort the dates to place them in chronological order.
2 Choose **Table**, **Sort…**	To open the Sort Text dialog box. By default, the paragraphs will be sorted by date in ascending, or chronological, order.
Click **OK**	To sort the selected text.
Deselect and observe the text	The dates are now arranged in chronological order.
3 Update and close the document	

Unit summary: Working with sections and columns

Topic A In this topic, you learned that you can use **sections** to format different parts of a document differently. You learned about the four types of section breaks. You learned how to insert section breaks by using the Break command. Then, you learned how to format sections.

Topic B In this topic, you learned how to format text into **columns** by using the Columns dialog box and the Columns button. You also learned how to insert a column break and how to change the spacing between columns. Then, you learned how to add a heading across columns. You also learned how to delete column breaks and remove columns.

Topic C In this topic, you learned how to add text and **headings** to columns. You also used the Sort Text dialog box to **sort text** in columns.

Independent practice activity

1 Open Hierarchy and save it as **My hierarchy**.

2 Starting immediately after the word "Hierarchy," format the text to the end of the document into three columns. (*Hint:* Select all text, starting from "President"; then display the column list, and select 3 Columns.)

3 Make the spacing between the columns 0.6" with a vertical line. (*Hint:* Use the Columns dialog box.)

4 Make the word "Hierarchy" a common heading for all three columns. (*Hint:* Center the word "Hierarchy.")

5 In the second column, insert a column break before "South region."

6 Hide all nonprinting characters.

7 Compare your work to Exhibit 1-5.

8 Update the document and close it. (Do not close Word.)

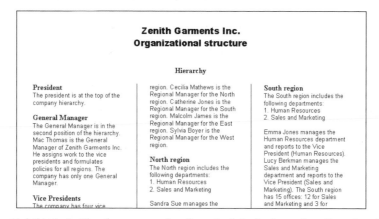

Exhibit 1-5: The document after Step 6 of the Independent Practice Activity

Review questions

1 Why would you want to create a new section?

2 What are the four types of section breaks?

3 By default, how many columns does a new document contain?

4 In the Break dialog box, which option should you choose if you want to create a newspaper-like layout?

   A Continuous section break

   B Text wrapping break

   C Column break

   D Next page section break

5 How do you position a heading across multiple columns?

6 What command is used to sort text in a column?

Unit 2

Formatting tables

Unit time: 40 minutes

Complete this unit, and you'll know how to:

A Modify a table by aligning text, merging cells, changing text orientation, and resizing rows and columns.

B Highlight table cells by adding borders and shading.

C Use the Table AutoFormat command to format tables, and set a default table format.

D Use the Tables and Borders toolbar to draw and modify tables.

Topic A: Table formatting basics

This topic covers the following Microsoft Office Specialist exam objectives.

#	Objective
WW03E-2-3	Modifying table formats by merging and/or splitting table cells
WW03E-2-3	Modifying text position and direction in a cell
WW03E-2-3	Modifying table properties (This objective is also covered in *Word 2003: Basic*, in the unit titled "Creating and managing tables.")

Aligning table text

Explanation

You can change a table's appearance by applying various formatting options. For example, you can align text in cells, merge cells, apply borders and shading to cells, and change text orientation.

When you enter text in a table cell, Word aligns the text to the upper-left corner by default. You can change text alignment by using the Tables and Borders toolbar. You can change the text alignment for the entire table or for selected cells.

To change the alignment of text within a cell:

1 Place the insertion point in the cell.

2 Choose View, Toolbars, Tables and Borders to display the Tables and Borders toolbar, shown in Exhibit 2-1. You can also click the Tables and Borders button on the Standard toolbar.

3 Click the down arrow next to the Alignment button to display the list of alignment options.

4 Select any of the alignment options.

You can also change text alignment either by using the Alignment buttons on the Formatting toolbar or by right-clicking the cell and choosing Cell Alignment from the shortcut menu. To change the text alignment for the entire table, select the table, right-click it, and choose Cell Alignment.

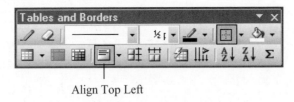

Align Top Left

Exhibit 2-1: The Tables and Borders toolbar

Do it!

A-1:   Aligning text in table cells

Here's how	Here's why
1 Open Report	(From the current unit folder.) In the table, the text entries and number values are right aligned.
Save the document as **My report**	
2 Select the second column	(Click in the selection area at the top of the "Employee name" column.) You'll left-align the values in this column.
3 Choose **View**, **Toolbars**, **Tables and Borders**	To display the Tables and Borders toolbar.
4 Click the arrow next to Align Top Left, as shown	
	(The Align Top Left button is the fourth button from the left in the second row on the Tables and Borders toolbar.) Clicking the arrow displays a list of alignment options.
From the list, select **Align Center Left**, as shown	
	To apply this setting to the selected column.
5 Apply Align Center Left to the third column	Select the "Employee code" column, and click the Align Center Left button.
6 Select the column headings **Qtr1**, **Qtr2**, and **Qtr3**	You'll center these three headings.
Display the list of alignment options	(On the Tables and Borders toolbar, click the down arrow next to the alignment button.) The button changes to reflect the most recently used alignment option.
From the list, select **Align Center**, as shown	

7 Apply Align Center to the
   quarterly numbers

   Deselect the columns

Qtr1	Qtr2	Qtr3
6,354	4,846	3,958
8,484	5,858	5,858
9,595	5,859	4,879

8 Update the document

Merging table cells

Explanation

You can merge cells when you want their contents to span more than one cell. Merging cells means combining two or more cells in the same row or column to form a single cell.

To merge cells in a table, select the cells you want to merge, and then choose Table, Merge Cells. You can also choose Merge Cells from the shortcut menu or click the Merge Cells button on the Tables and Borders toolbar.

Splitting table cells

You can also split a cell into multiple columns or multiple rows. To split a cell:

1   Place the insertion point in the cell you want to split.

2   Choose Table, Split Cells, or click the Split Cells button on the Tables and Borders toolbar, to open the Split Cells dialog box.

3   In the Split Cells dialog box, enter the number of columns and rows you want to use.

4   Click OK.

Do it! **A-2: Merging table cells**

Here's how	Here's why
1 Select the first column	Click in the column, and choose Table, Select, Column.
2 Right-click the selection	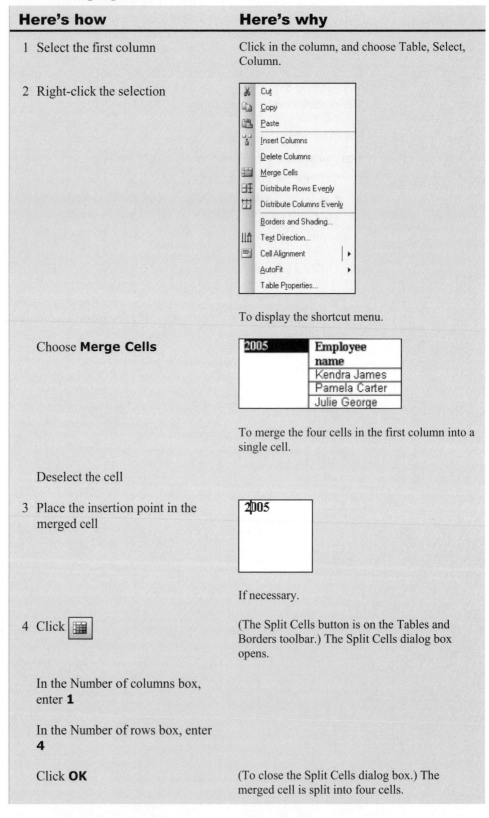

To display the shortcut menu.

Choose **Merge Cells**

To merge the four cells in the first column into a single cell.

Deselect the cell

3 Place the insertion point in the merged cell

If necessary.

4 Click [ ]

(The Split Cells button is on the Tables and Borders toolbar.) The Split Cells dialog box opens.

In the Number of columns box, enter **1**

In the Number of rows box, enter **4**

Click **OK**

(To close the Split Cells dialog box.) The merged cell is split into four cells.

5 Select the first column	You'll merge the cells again.
Merge the cells	Right-click, and choose Merge Cells.
Deselect the cell	The cells are merged into a single cell.
6 Update the document	

Changing the orientation of text

Explanation

To improve the readability of data in a table, you might need to change its orientation. By default, Word aligns text horizontally. To change the orientation of text in a table:

1   Select the cell(s) whose orientation you want to change.

2   Choose Format, Text Direction to open the Text Direction - Table Cell dialog box, shown in Exhibit 2-2. You can also open the dialog box by right-clicking the selected cell(s) and choosing Text Direction from the shortcut menu.

3   Select the desired orientation.

4   Click OK.

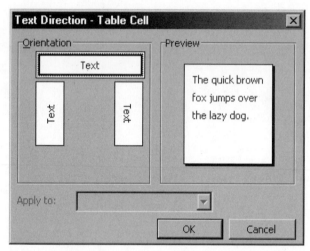

Exhibit 2-2: The Text Direction - Table Cell dialog box

Do it!

A-3:   Changing text orientation

Here's how	Here's why
1 Place the insertion point in the first cell of the table	If necessary.
2 Choose **Format**, **Text Direction...**	To open the Text Direction - Table Cell dialog box.
3 Under Orientation, select the indicated option	

This setting positions the text vertically. The Preview area displays an example of how the text will look.

Click **OK**	To apply the new orientation. Notice that the alignment buttons on the Formatting toolbar change accordingly.
4 Click [⦀]	(On the formatting toolbar.) To center the text vertically within the cell.
5 Update the document	

Resizing rows

Explanation

You can change the size of table rows by dragging the cell boundaries or by using the Table Properties dialog box. Usually, you need to change row height so that the data fits well in the cell.

To change the row height, point to the row boundary, and when the pointer becomes a double-headed arrow, drag up or down. You can also use the Table Properties dialog box to change the row height to a specific value.

To specify a row's height:

1 Place the insertion point in the row whose height you want to change.
2 Choose Table, Table Properties to open the Table Properties dialog box.
3 Click the Row tab.
4 If necessary, check Specify height.
5 By using the spinner controls, enter the row height.
6 Click OK.

Do it!

A-4: Changing row height

Here's how	Here's why
1 Select the entire table	Click the table-move handle to quickly select the entire table.
Right-click the table	To display the shortcut menu.
2 Choose **Table Properties...**	To open the Table Properties dialog box.
3 Click the **Row** tab	
4 Check **Specify height**	
5 Edit the Specify height box to read **0.5"**	(Use the spinner controls.) To specify a row height of 0.5 inch.
Click **OK**	To apply the new setting.
6 Deselect the table	Click anywhere outside the table. The height of the rows has increased to .5".
Update the document	

Distributing rows and columns evenly across a table

Explanation

You might want to space the rows and columns evenly across a table. To do this, choose Table, AutoFit, and the relevant command.

- To evenly distribute columns, select the columns, and choose Table, AutoFit, Distribute Columns Evenly.
- To evenly distribute rows, select the rows, and choose Table, AutoFit, Distribute Rows Evenly.

You can also use the Tables and Borders toolbar buttons or the shortcut menu to distribute rows and columns evenly.

	Employee name	Employee code	Qtr1	Qtr2	Qtr3
2005	Kendra James	16	6,354	4,846	3,958
	Pamela Carter	25	8,484	5,858	5,858
	Julie George	29	9,595	5,859	4,879

Exhibit 2-3: The table after Step 4 of the activity

Do it!   ## A-5:   Distributing columns evenly across a table

Here's how	Here's why
1 Point to the right border of the first column	 **Employee name** Kendra James Pamela Carter 2005 (The shape of the pointer changes.) You'll change the width of the first column.
2 Drag the border to the left as shown	 **Employee name** Kendra James Pamela Carter 2005 To decrease the width of the first column.
3 Select the second and third columns	You'll distribute the two columns evenly within the table.
4 Click ⊞	(The Distribute Columns Evenly button is on the Tables and Borders toolbar.) To create two equal-width columns. The column headings now fit on one line.
Deselect the columns	The "Employee name" and "Employee code" columns have equal width, as shown in Exhibit 2-3.
5 Update the document	

Topic B: Borders and shading

This topic covers the following Microsoft Office Specialist exam objective.

#	Objective
WW03S-2-1	Modifying table borders and shading

Table borders

Explanation

After you've created a table, you can apply borders and shading to highlight different portions. Word provides multiple ways to apply borders and shading. The Tables and Borders toolbar contains buttons specifically for this purpose. You can also use the Borders and Shading command in the Format menu to open the Borders and Shading dialog box, shown in Exhibit 2-4. You can apply formatting options, such as shadows, 3-D effects, and colors, by using this dialog box.

You can add borders to a cell, a row, a column, or an entire table. To apply borders:

1 Choose Format, Borders and Shading to open the Borders and Shading dialog box. Verify that the Borders tab is activated.
2 Under Setting, select the type of border you want to apply.
3 From the Style list, select a line style.
4 From the Color list, select a line color.
5 From the Width list, select the line width for the border.
6 From the Apply to list, select the area to which you want to apply the border (paragraph, cell, or table).
7 Click OK.

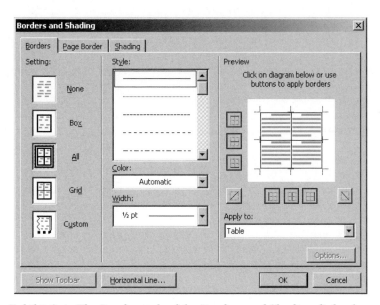

Exhibit 2-4: The Borders tab of the Borders and Shading dialog box

Do it!   **B-1:   Adding borders to a table**

Here's how	Here's why
1 Select the table	
Right-click the table	To display the shortcut menu.
2 Choose **Borders and Shading...**	To open the Borders and Shading dialog box.
Verify that the Borders tab is activated	You'll apply a border to the table by using the options in this tab.
3 Under Setting, select **Box**	To add a box border around the table.
4 From the Width list, select **3 pt**	To specify the width of the border.
5 In the Apply to list, verify that Table is selected	
Click **OK**	To close the dialog box and apply a 3-point box around the table.
6 Deselect the table	
7 Update the document	

Shading table cells

Explanation

You might want to highlight some sections of a table to draw the reader's attention to them. You can apply shading to highlight sections of a table. You can apply shading either to the entire table or to specific cells. To do so:

1 Select the cells you want to shade.
2 Open the Borders and Shading dialog box.
3 Click the Shading tab.
4 Specify the color and pattern.
5 Click OK.

	Employee name	Employee code	Qtr1	Qtr2	Qtr3
2005	Kendra James	16	6,354	4,846	3,958
	Pamela Carter	25	8,484	5,858	5,858
	Julie George	29	9,595	5,859	4,879

Exhibit 2-5: The shaded cells in a table

Do it!

B-2: Shading table cells

Here's how	Here's why
1 Select the first row	(Use the selection bar to select the row.) You'll shade this row. The first column is part of this row because it contains a single merged cell.
2 On the Tables and Borders toolbar, display the Shading Color list	
Click Gray-25% as indicated	No Fill Gray-25%
	To select the gray shading.
Click **OK**	To close the dialog box and to apply the shading to the selected row.
3 Deselect the row	The first row and the first column are shaded in gray, as shown in Exhibit 2-5.
4 Update the document	

Topic C: Table AutoFormat

This topic covers the following Microsoft Office Specialist exam objective.

#	Objective
WW03S-2-1	Applying pre-defined formats to tables (e.g., AutoFormats)

The Table AutoFormat dialog box

Explanation

Word provides 45 pre-defined table formats, also known as *AutoFormats*. Each AutoFormat contains a collection of formatting options, such as shading, borders, and 3D effects, which you can apply to a table. When you apply an AutoFormat, it overrides any current table formatting.

To access Word's pre-defined table formats, choose Table, Table AutoFormat to open the Table AutoFormat dialog box, shown in Exhibit 2-6. Or, you can click the Table AutoFormat button on the Tables and Borders toolbar. You can then select a format from the Table styles list. The other options in the dialog box help you modify the format of the table.

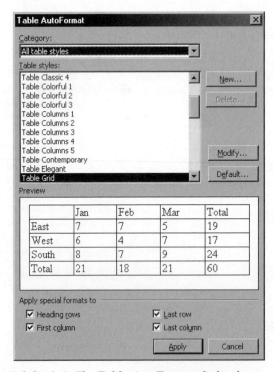

Exhibit 2-6: The Table AutoFormat dialog box

Do it!

C-1:   Using AutoFormat to format a table

Here's how	Here's why
1 Place the insertion point anywhere in the table	
2 Click 🔲	(The Table AutoFormat button is on the Tables and Borders toolbar.) To open the Table AutoFormat dialog box.
3 From the Table styles list, select a style of your choice	The Preview area displays how your table would look with the selected style.
4 Explore some of the other AutoFormats	Select them and observe the Preview area.
5 Select **Table Classic 3**	
Click **Apply**	To close the dialog box and apply the Table Classic 3 style to the table. The previously applied border and shading have been replaced by the AutoFormat.
6 Update the document	

Setting the default table format

Explanation

You can select a table style from the Table AutoFormat dialog box and set that style as the default by clicking the Default button. This way, whenever you want to store data in tables, you won't need to spend time choosing a style or searching for it. You can set a style as the default table style for the current document only or for all documents based on the Normal template.

Do it!

C-2:   Setting the default table format

Here's how	Here's why
1 Open the Table AutoFormat dialog box	(Click the Table AutoFormat button on the Tables and Borders toolbar.) In the Table styles list, Table Classic 3 is selected. You'll set this as the default table style.
2 Click **Default**	

Default Table Style ☒

Style: **Table Classic 3**

Do you want to set this style as the default table style for:

⦿ This document only?

○ All documents based on the Normal template?

[OK]   [Cancel]

	(To open the Default Table Style dialog box.) By default, the option This document only is selected. With this setting, the selected style will be set as the default for the current document only.
Click **OK**	

3 Place the insertion point at the end
of the document

On the Tables and Borders
toolbar, click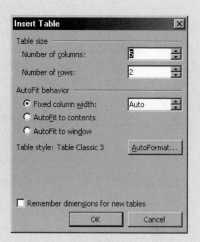

To open the Insert Table dialog box. Under
AutoFit behavior, the table style is set to Table
Classic 3. You'll insert this table to see how the
default table style is applied to the table.

Click **OK**

To insert a table with the Table Classic 3 style.

4 Update the document

Topic D: Drawing tables

Explanation

The Table menu includes two commands you can use to create a new table: Insert Table and Draw Table. The advantage of drawing a table is that you can create rows of different heights, vary the number of columns in a row, and create nested tables (tables within tables). When you choose to draw a table, the pointer changes to the shape of a pencil. When you choose to modify a table, the pointer changes to an eraser.

Using the Draw Table button

The Tables and Borders toolbar contains the tools for drawing tables. To display this toolbar, choose View, Toolbars, Tables and Borders, or use the Table, Draw Table command. When you use the Draw Table button, the mouse pointer changes to a pencil. To draw a table:

1 Display the Tables and Borders toolbar.
2 Click the Draw Table button.
3 Drag to draw the outline of the table.
4 Drag to draw the rows and columns of the table.

Do it!   **D-1:   Drawing a table**

Here's how	Here's why
1 Place the insertion point at the end of the document	
2 Click	(The Draw Table button is on the Tables and Borders toolbar.) The pointer changes to the shape of a pencil.
3 Drag to create a rectangle, as shown	This rectangle defines the outside border of the table. The new table contains a 3 pt. border because that was set earlier.
4 From the upper horizontal line of the table, draw a line, as shown	To draw the first column.
5 Draw a horizontal line, as shown	To start dividing the right side of the table into rows.
6 Draw another horizontal line, as shown	To create three rows.
7 Update the document	

Erasing lines in a table

Explanation

If you want to remove a column or row from a table you have drawn, you can do so by using the Eraser button on the Tables and Borders toolbar. To do this, click the button and then use the mouse to erase the dividing lines.

Do it!

D-2: Using the Eraser button to modify a table

Here's how	Here's why
1 Click	(The Eraser button is on the Tables and Borders toolbar.) The pointer changes to the shape of an eraser.
2 Click any line in the table	(On the table you created in the previous activity.) To erase it.
Erase the table	Clicking all the lines.
3 Close the Tables and Borders toolbar	Click the Close button in the upper-right corner of the Tables and Borders toolbar.
4 Update and close the document	

Unit summary: Formatting tables

Topic A

In this topic, you learned how to **align text** in table cells and how to change the text orientation. You also learned how to merge **table cells**, change row heights, and distribute rows and columns evenly across a table.

Topic B

In this topic, you learned that you can apply **borders** and **shading** to a table by using the Borders and Shading dialog box.

Topic C

In this topic, you used the **AutoFormat** feature to quickly change the appearance of a table. You observed the different types of built-in formats, and you set a new default **table style** for a document.

Topic D

In this topic, you created a table with irregular-sized cells by using the **Draw Table** button. Then, you deleted columns and rows by using the Eraser button on the Tables and Borders toolbar.

Independent practice activity

1 Open Sales and save it as **My sales**.

2 Apply the Align Bottom Left format to all rows containing values. (*Hint:* Use the Tables and Borders toolbar.)

3 Shade the first row of the table in blue.

4 Set the row height of the table to 0.2".

5 Compare your work with Exhibit 2-7.

6 Set Table List 7 as the default table style for the document.

7 Create a table with the default table style and with three rows and four columns.

8 Close the Tables and Borders toolbar.

9 Update and close the document.

Outlander Spices
Yearly sales report of Northern region

Year	Qtr1	Qtr2	Qtr3	Qtr4
2000	21,333	16,584	14,569	14,658
2001	22,050	17,465	16,935	17,226
2002	14,563	15,478	18,756	17,563
2003	17,895	19,872	19,653	19,845
2004	22,156	14,235	15,698	21,036
2005	20,789	12,458	13,698	18,654

Exhibit 2-7: The document after Step 4 of the Independent Practice Activity

Review questions

1 What is the definition of merging cells?

2 What command is used to change the orientation of text in a cell?

3 Name the two methods that can be used to resize a row.

4 Which command is used to distribute columns evenly in a table?

   A Table, Columns, Match width.

   B Table, Distribute Columns Evenly

   C Table, AutoFormat, Distribute Columns Evenly

   D Table, AutoFit, Distribute Columns Evenly

5 Which command is used to highlight cells in a table?

6 What is one potential disadvantage to applying a table AutoFormat?

Unit 3

Working with Excel data

Unit time: 40 minutes

Complete this unit, and you'll know how to:

A Import data, format data in tables, and create and modify charts.

B Use formulas to perform calculations in a table.

C Link and embed Excel data in Word.

Topic A: Importing data and creating charts

This topic covers the following Microsoft Office Specialist exam objectives.

#	Objective
WW03S-1-5	Creating and modifying charts and diagrams (This objective is also covered in the unit titled "Working with graphics and objects.")
WW03E-1-5	Creating and revising charts using data from other sources (e.g., Excel)

Importing data from Excel

Explanation

You might have some sales data stored in an Excel file and want to present it in a Word document. You can import data from an Excel worksheet by opening the Excel file in Word. When you do so, the imported data is converted to a Word table. You can edit, sort, and format the imported data just as you would in any Word table. You can also create a chart based on this imported data.

To import data from Excel:

1 In Word, click Insert Database on the Database toolbar to open the Database dialog box. The Database dialog box helps you import data from different data sources, such as Excel or Access.

2 Click Get Data to open the Select Data Source dialog box.

3 Navigate to and select the Excel file you want to import.

4 Click Open to display the Select Table dialog box.

5 From the Name list, select the desired sheet.

6 Click OK to return to the Database dialog box.

7 Click Insert Data to open the Insert Data dialog box. Here, you can choose to insert all or some of the data.

8 Click OK.

Do it!

A-1: Importing data from an Excel worksheet

Here's how	Here's why
1 Create a new document, and save it as **My quarterly**	(In the current unit folder.) You'll import an Excel worksheet into this document.
2 Choose **View**, **Toolbars**, **Database**	To display the Database toolbar.
3 Click [icon]	(The Insert Database button is on the Database toolbar.) To open the Database dialog box.
4 Click **Get Data**	To open the Select Data Source dialog box.
Navigate to the current unit folder	
5 Select **Quarterly sales**	You'll import a worksheet from this Excel workbook into the Word document.
Click **Open**	The Select Table dialog box opens.
Verify that Employee Sales$ is selected	Under Type, the type of the data is given as table. Because the data in the Excel worksheet is in columnar format, the data is imported into Word as a table.
Click **OK**	To close the Select Table dialog box.
6 Click **Insert Data**	To open the Insert Data dialog box. You can choose to insert all or some of the data records. By default, All is selected.
Click **OK**	To import the Employee Sales worksheet as a table into your Word document.
Update the document	

Formatting data in a table

Explanation

Because imported Excel data becomes a Word table, you can format it like any other table. You can also use the sort feature to organize table information in a particular order. To do so, select the rows to be organized, and choose Table, Sort to open the Sort dialog box, shown in Exhibit 3-1. By default, the selected data is sorted alphabetically in ascending order. You can also choose to sort numerically or chronologically.

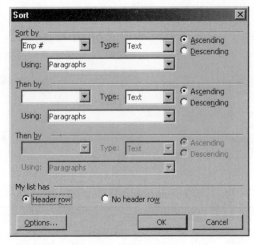

Exhibit 3-1: The Sort dialog box

Do it!   **A-2:   Formatting data in a table**

Here's how	Here's why
1 Select the text in the first row	
Click B	(The Bold button is on the Formatting toolbar.) To apply bold formatting to the column headings.
2 Select all rows in the table	You need to include the heading row because Word uses it to determine your sorting options.
Choose **Table, Sort...**	To open the Sort dialog box. By default, the table will be sorted by column 1, which is employee number, in ascending order.
Select **Header row**	My list has ⊙ Header row ○ No header row
	(If necessary.) To indicate that the table contains a row with headings.
Click **OK**	To sort the selected data by the Emp # column.
3 Deselect the table	The data in the table is sorted in ascending order.
4 Update the document	

Creating a chart from table data

Explanation

Charts represent data graphically. To create a chart, select the table data that you want to represent as a chart. Then, choose Insert, Picture, Chart. The chart appears below the Word table, and the data appears in a datasheet window. A *datasheet* is a series of columns and rows, as shown in Exhibit 3-2. The datasheet is linked to the chart. When you modify the contents of the datasheet, the chart is updated automatically.

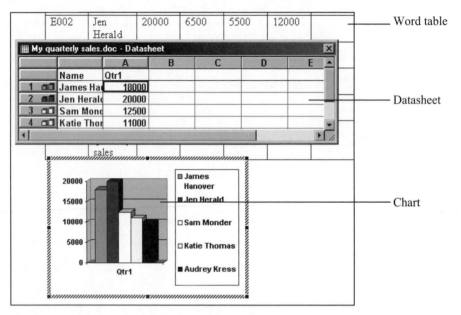

Exhibit 3-2: A sample datasheet and chart

Do it!

A-3: Creating a chart

Here's how	Here's why
1 In the table, select the Name and Qtr1 columns	You'll create a chart showing each person's Qtr1 sales.
2 Choose **Insert**, **Picture**, **Chart**	To insert a chart, as shown in Exhibit 3-2. The chart is inserted below the table. A datasheet with the chart data also appears.
3 Click outside the datasheet	To close the datasheet.
4 Update the document	

Modifying charts

Explanation

The chart is an object in the Word document. You can click the chart object to select it and work with the chart as a whole. To modify the chart elements, you need to double-click the chart to open it. When you do this, the menu bar includes Data and Chart menus, and the Standard toolbar contains chart-related buttons.

You can select from a variety of chart types, such as Column and Bar. Each chart type also has sub-types. After you create a chart, you can change its type. To modify the chart type, choose Chart, Chart Type. From the Chart type list, select the desired chart; click OK. You can also add legends, titles, and data labels to the chart. In addition, you can modify its border and size.

The following table describes some of the elements of a chart:

Element	Description
Chart title	The identifying text at the top of the chart.
Category (X) axis	The horizontal axis, which contains the categories.
Value (Y) axis	The vertical axis, which contains the data that is charted.
Legend	The text that explains the values contained in the data series.
Grid lines	The lines that help you determine the value of a plotted point.

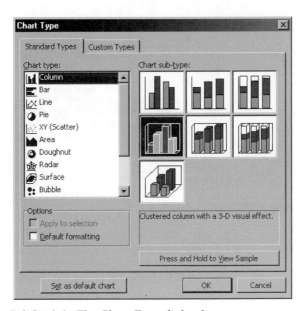

Exhibit 3-3: The Chart Type dialog box

A-4:   Modifying a chart

Here's how	Here's why
1 Double-click the chart	The menu bar expands to include the Data and Chart menus. The Standard toolbar also expands to include chart-related buttons. The datasheet appears in case you want to change the values that were used to create the chart.
2 Choose **Chart**, **Chart Type...**	To open the Chart Type dialog box, shown in Exhibit 3-3. By default, the Standard Types tab is activated.
From the Chart type list, select **Bar**	
	To change the chart to a bar chart. For each chart type, there are sub-types that provide slightly different options, such as 3-D effects.
Click **OK**	
	To apply the selected chart type. The data is now represented as a clustered bar chart. The Value axis appears in increments of 10,000.
3 Verify that the chart is selected	You'll resize the chart to make it clearer.

4 Along the right border of the chart, point to the center sizing handle as shown

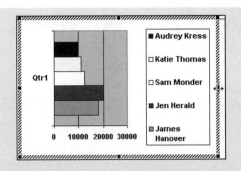

The pointer becomes a double-headed arrow.

5 Drag the border to the right

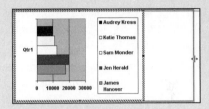

(Drag to the right until the border is aligned with the right side of the table.) The quarterly sales values are in increments of 5,000.

Close the datasheet

6 Update the document

Topic B: Performing calculations in tables

This topic covers the following Microsoft Office Specialist exam objective.

#	Objective
WW03E-2-2	Using formulas in tables

The Formula dialog box

Explanation

You can perform various calculations in rows and columns by using formulas. A *formula* is used to perform arithmetic operations, such as calculating an average or a sum. You can also copy formulas from one cell to another in a table.

You can create formulas by using the Formula dialog box, shown in Exhibit 3-4. To open the Formula dialog box, choose Table, Formula. In the Formula dialog box:

- A formula is always preceded by an equal sign (=).
- From the Number format list, you can select the format you want the result in, such as currency or percentage.
- From the Paste function list, you can select the function that you want to use in the formula. A *function* is a built-in formula that you can use to perform mathematical calculations. For example, the SUM function adds the numbers in the selected cells. Other functions include MAX, MIN, and AVG.

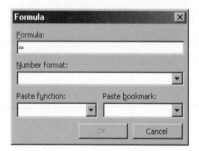

Exhibit 3-4: The Formula dialog box

In Word documents, formulas are treated as fields. When information is subject to change, a *field* is used as a placeholder for that information. For example, a formula that totals a column of numbers is based on the values in the column. If any number in the column changes, the formula needs to reflect the change. In such situations, fields provide the best way to store and display dynamic information.

Calculating totals in rows and columns

You use the SUM function to calculate totals in rows and columns. If the insertion point is in a table containing a series of numbers, the SUM function appears in the Formula dialog box by default. If the insertion point is placed below a cell containing a number, the Formula box will contain =SUM(ABOVE), which adds the numbers in the column. If there are no numbers above the cell, the formula box will contain =SUM(LEFT), which adds the numbers in the row to the left of the formula. By default, the formula result will have the same formatting as the numbers used in the calculation.

Do it!

B-1: Calculating totals

Here's how	Here's why
1 At the bottom of the table, insert a new row In the Name column, enter **Totals**	
2 Move to the last cell in the Qtr1 column	
3 Choose **Table, Formula...**	To open the Formula dialog box.
4 In the Formula box, verify that =SUM(ABOVE) appears	Formula: =SUM(ABOVE) Because you selected the last cell of a column of numbers, Word assumes that you want to add up those numbers.
From the Number format list, select **$#,##0.00;($#,##0.00)**	Formula Formula: =SUM(ABOVE) Number format: #,##0 #,##0.00 $#,##0.00;($#,##0.00) 0 0% 0.00 0.00% This is a currency format.
Click **OK**	To enter the formula. The sum is automatically calculated.
5 Click **$71,500.00**	The gray shading on the sum indicates that this formula has been entered as a field.
6 Click the cell below "Total yearly sales"	You'll calculate the total sales for James Hanover.
7 Open the Formula dialog box	(Choose Table, Formula.) The =SUM(LEFT) function appears in the Formula box. This formula adds up the numbers to the left of the selected cell.
From the Number format list, select the currency format	$#,##0.00;($#,##0.00)
Click **OK**	To calculate the row total. The yearly sales total for James Hanover is $45,700.00.
8 Update the document	

Copying formulas

Explanation

You can easily copy a formula from one field to another. However, when you copy a formula, the cells that the formula refers to are now different. In Word, you must manually update the formula so that it refers to the correct cells.

To copy and update a formula:

1   Copy the field that contains the formula.

2   Paste the field into a new cell. You'll see that the original calculated value is maintained, indicating that the cell reference has not been updated.

3   Right-click the cell to display the shortcut menu, and then choose Update Field to update the cell references. You can also press F9 to update cell references.

Do it!

B-2:   Copying a formula

Here's how	Here's why
1 Select the formula for James Hanover's total yearly sales	<table><tr><td>Qtr4</td><td>Total yearly sales</td></tr><tr><td>9000</td><td>$45,700.00</td></tr></table>
	You'll copy this formula to total the other rows.
Copy the formula	You can click the Copy button, press Ctrl+C, or choose Copy from the shortcut menu.
2 Place the insertion point in the cell for Jen Herald's total yearly sales	<table><tr><td>Qtr4</td><td>Total yearly sales</td></tr><tr><td>9000</td><td>$45,700.00</td></tr><tr><td>12000</td><td></td></tr></table>
Paste the formula	<table><tr><td>Qtr4</td><td>Total yearly sales</td></tr><tr><td>9000</td><td>$45,700.00</td></tr><tr><td>12000</td><td>$45,700.00</td></tr></table>
	The original calculated value is maintained, indicating that the cell references have not been updated.
3 Place the insertion point as shown	<table><tr><td>12000</td><td>$45,700.00</td></tr></table>
	The field shading needs to be visible for you to see the correct shortcut menu in the next step.
Right-click the field	

4 Choose **Update Field**

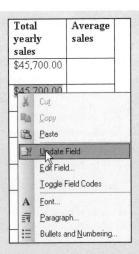

To update the formula in the cell so that it contains the proper cell references. The value in the cell now displays the correct sum of $44,000.00.

5 Calculate the total yearly sales for the remaining rows

Copy and paste the formulas, and then choose Update Field (or press F9) to recalculate the totals.

6 Calculate the total quarterly sales for Qtr2, Qtr3, and Qtr4

You can enter the formulas, or copy, paste, and update the fields.

Adjust the column width to fit the totals

Select the table, and choose Table, AutoFit, AutoFit to Window.

7 Update the document

Creating formulas

Explanation

To create a formula, open the Formula dialog box, select a function from the Paste Function drop-down list, and then enter the appropriate cell references. Formulas must be formatted in this order: an equal sign (=), followed by the function name and the range of cells that will be used in the calculation. When creating a formula, you use the minus sign (-) for subtraction and the front slash (/) for division.

You also need to specify the cells that you want to include in the calculation. A comma (,) separates individual cells in a formula—for example: A1, B6, C3. The letter in the cell reference represents the column, and the number represents the row. To include a range of cells in a formula, use a colon to separate the first cell reference from the last reference of the range. For example, to cover a range that spans from cell B2 to cell D2, you would enter B2:D2.

C2   F2   =AVERAGE(D2:F2)

Emp #	Name	Qtr1	Qtr2	Qtr3	Qtr4	Total yearly sales	Average sales
E001	James Hanover	18000	9000	9700	9000	$45,700.00	$11,425.00
E002	Jen Herald	20000	6500	5500	12000	$44,000.00	
E003	Sam Monder	12500	7000	11000	8800	$39,300.00	
E004	Katie Thomas	11000	8500	7700	7000	$34,200.00	
E005	Audrey Kress	10000	5000	9000	15000	$39,000.00	
Totals		$71,500.00	$36,000.00	$42,900.00	$51,800.00		

Exhibit 3-5: Using cell references in formulas

Do it!

B-3: Creating a formula

Here's how	Here's why
1 Place the insertion point in the cell below "Average sales" as shown	<table><tr><td>Total yearly sales</td><td>Average sales</td></tr><tr><td>$45,700.00</td><td></td></tr></table>
	You'll calculate the average yearly sales for James Hanover.
2 Choose **Table**, **Formula...**	By default, Word assumes that you want to add the numbers to the left of the selected cell.
3 In the Formula box, select **=SUM(LEFT)**	You'll replace this SUM formula with an AVG one.
Enter **=**	All formulas must begin with an equal sign.
4 From the Paste function list, select **AVERAGE**	Paste function: ABS AND AVERAGE COUNT DEFINED FALSE IF INT
	The Formula box displays =AVERAGE().
5 Verify that the insertion point is between the parentheses	You'll insert the cell references in the formula.
Enter **C2:F2**	To create a formula that averages the four quarterly sales figures for James Hanover, as illustrated in Exhibit 3-5.
Select the currency format	From the Number format list.
Click **OK**	James Hanover's average yearly sales total is $11,425.00, as shown in Exhibit 3-5.
6 Update and close the document	

Topic C: Linking and embedding data

Explanation

If you want to use Excel to edit the data you import into Word, you need to either link or embed the Excel data into your document. Linking and embedding are methods used to insert Excel data into a Word document as objects. Linking and embedding help you update the imported data by using the Excel interface and commands without leaving the Word environment.

Embedding Excel data

An *embedded* worksheet is stored in the Word document and does not maintain links to the original Excel file. As a result, any changes made in the original Excel file will *not* be reflected in the data embedded in the Word document.

To embed data from an Excel worksheet:

1. Place the insertion point in the Word document.
2. Choose Insert, Object to open the Object dialog box.
3. Click the Create from File tab.
4. In the File name box, enter the path of the file you want to import. You can also use the Browse button to navigate to the file.
5. Click OK to close the dialog box and insert the data into your document.

When you use the Insert, Object command to embed Excel data, the entire contents of the worksheet are inserted into your document. At times, you might want to insert only a portion of the worksheet. In that case, use the Paste Special feature to insert only the data you need.

Editing embedded data

You can modify the embedded data without leaving the Word environment. If you click the embedded object, you can resize it by dragging the selection handles. To open the object in edit mode, double-click the embedded object. As shown in Exhibit 3-6, the embedded object appears in its source application, such as Excel. In addition, corresponding menus and toolbar buttons are available.

	A	B	C	D	E
1	Outlander Spices				
2	Sales Report of Northern Region				
3					
4	Quarterly sales				
5					
6		Qtr1	Qtr2	Qtr3	Qtr4
7	Kendra James	$6,354	$4,846	$3,958	$8,284
8	Pamela Carter	$8,484	$5,858	$5,858	$4,555
9	Julie George	$9,595	$5,859	$4,879	$3,432
10	Henry Jones	$6,350	$5,930	$5,550	$7,660
11	Alan Knight	$4,600	$5,200	$4,900	$1,550

Exhibit 3-6: The embedded data in edit mode

Do it!

C-1: Embedding Excel data in Word

Here's how	Here's why
1 Create a new Word document, and save it as **My embedded file**	(In the current unit folder.) You'll embed the Northern region sales report in this document.
2 Choose **Insert**, **Object...**	To open the Object dialog box.
Activate the **Create from File** tab	
3 Click **Browse**	To open the Browse dialog box.
Navigate to the current unit folder	If necessary.
Select **Northern sales**	
Click **Insert**	

Object

Create New | Create from File

File name:

C:\Student Data\Unit_03\Northern sales.xls

	To close the Browse dialog box and enter Northern sales.xls in the File name box.
4 Click **OK**	To close the Object dialog box and embed the data from the Excel file in the Word document. Unlike imported data, this is an object, not a Word table.
5 Double-click the embedded sheet	To open the sheet in edit mode. The sheet appears as it opens in Excel; the Sales sheet is activated. You can edit the data now.
Observe the Standard toolbar	

A1   ▾   *fx* Outlander Spices

	The Standard toolbar expands to include Excel-related buttons. You can also see the Formula bar, which you can use to edit formulas.
6 Select the column headings **Qtr1**, **Qtr2**, **Qtr3**, and **Qtr4**	
Click ≡	(The Center button is on the Formatting toolbar.) To center the column headings.
7 Deselect the object	Click outside the object.
8 Update the document	

Linking Excel data in Word

Explanation

When you *link* an Excel worksheet to a Word document, any change made in the original Excel file will be reflected in the data linked to the Word document. To link data from an Excel worksheet:

1 Place the insertion point in the Word document.
2 Choose Insert, Object to open the Object dialog box.
3 In the File name box, enter the path of the file you want to link. You can also use the Browse button to navigate to the file.
4 Check Link to file.
5 Click OK to close the dialog box and to insert the data into the document.

Do it!

C-2: Linking Excel data in Word

Here's how	Here's why
1 Place the insertion point below the embedded object	You might want to insert a few blank lines to separate the objects.
2 Choose **Insert**, **Object...**	To open the Object dialog box.
Activate the **Create from File** tab	
3 Browse to insert Northern sales	Click Browse, navigate to the current unit folder, select Northern sales, and click Insert.
Check **Link to file**	

File name:

C:\Student Data\Unit_03\Northern sales.xls   Browse...

☑ Link to file
☐ Display as ic

Result

Inserts the contents of the file into your document and creates a shortcut to the source file. Changes to the source file will be reflected in your document.

	To create a link to the original Excel file. The Result area explains that any changes in the source file are reflected in your document because of the link.
4 Click **OK**	To close the Object dialog box. The Northern sales file is inserted as an object in the Word document.
5 Double-click the linked sheet	Because the Northern sales sheet is linked, Excel opens when you double-click the object.
6 Edit the B11 cell to read **$4,000**	To change Alan Knight's Qtr1 sales to $4,000.
Press (↵ ENTER)	

7 Switch to Word

   Observe the linked data   The change made in the Excel file is reflected in
                                              the linked data in the Word document. Alan
                                              Knight's Qtr1 sales amount is $4,000.

8 Observe the embedded data   The changes made in the Excel file are not
                                              reflected in the embedded data. Alan Knight's
                                              Qtr1 sales remains at $4,600.

9 Close Excel without saving your
   changes

   Update and close the document

Unit summary: Working with Excel data

Topic E
In this topic, you learned how to **import data** from an Excel worksheet. You also formatted and sorted the imported data in the tables. In addition, you learned how to create and modify **charts**.

Topic F
In this topic, you learned how to **perform calculations** in tables. You also used the Formula dialog box to calculate totals in rows and columns. In addition, you learned how to create and copy **formulas**.

Topic G
In this topic, you learned how to **link** and **embed** Excel data in Word. You also learned how to edit the embedded data. In addition, you examined what happens to the linked data in a document when you edit the original Excel file.

Independent practice activity

1 Import the data from the Excel file Total sales into a new Word document. (Only Sheet 1 of the Excel file contains data.)

2 Save the document as **My total sales**.

3 Sort the table by year in ascending order. (*Hint:* While sorting, select all rows except the last one.)

4 Center the headings and make them bold.

5 Right-align the data in the Sales column.

6 Resize the width of the columns according to the size of the data.

7 Edit the last cell of the first column to read **Total**.

8 In the last cell, enter a formula to calculate the total.

9 Change the formula to the currency format.

10 Compare your work with Exhibit 3-7.

11 Link the Excel file Total sales to this document. (*Hint:* Use the Object dialog box.)

12 Close the Database toolbar.

13 Update and close the document.

Year	Sales
1997	89021
1998	21333
1999	14563
2000	12987
2001	17895
2002	125467
2003	32765
2004	65430
2005	65400
Total	$444,861.00

Exhibit 3-7: The document after Step 9 of the Independent Practice Activity

Review questions

1 How do you import Excel data into a Word document?

2 Once imported into Word, which of the following can be done to the data?

    A Apply table formatting

    B Sort the data

    C Create a chart from table data

    D All of the above

3 Which command is used to create a chart from table data?

4 Name a few of the standard chart types.

5 How do you know that Word considers a chart to be an object?

6 What must all formulas start with?

7 Which is the best definition of a function?

    A A complicated formula.

    B A mathematical calculation.

    C A built-in formula.

    D A series of calculations.

8 What is the procedure to total numbers in a table column?

9 After copying or moving formulas, how do you guarantee that the formula is still calculating the intended values?

10 What is the difference between linked and embedded data in a Word document?

Unit 4

Working with styles

Unit time: 40 minutes

Complete this unit, and you'll know how to:

A Use styles to apply multiple formats.

B Modify and delete styles.

C Use Outline view, the Document Map pane, and thumbnails to navigate through a large document.

Topic A: Creating styles

This topic covers the following Microsoft Office Specialist exam objectives.

#	Objective
WW03S-3-1	Applying styles to and clearing styles from text, tables, and lists (This objective is also covered in Topic B.)
WW03E-1-1	Creating an applying custom styles for text, tables, and lists

Applying styles

Explanation

Styles are named sets of formats that define the appearance of recurring text components, such as headings or captions. By using a style, you can apply several formats in one step. For example, if you want all of the section titles in a document to be 16pt, Arial, and centered, you can save and apply this combination of formats as a style. Styles can help you maintain formatting consistency within and among documents.

You can apply a style to selected text in one of two ways. Either select the desired style from the Style list on the Formatting toolbar, or use the Styles and Formatting task pane.

To apply a style by using the Styles and Formatting task pane:

1 Select the text to which you want to apply a style.

2 Choose Format, Styles and Formatting, or click the Styles and Formatting button on the Formatting toolbar, to display the Styles and Formatting task pane, shown in Exhibit 4-1.

3 From the Pick formatting to apply list, select the desired style.

Word provides several predefined styles. For example, you can apply the Heading 1 style to format selected text as a heading. By default, when you create a new document, Word applies the Normal style to the entire document.

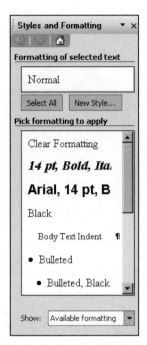

Exhibit 4-1: The Styles and Formatting task pane

Do it!

A-1: Applying a style

Here's how	Here's why
1 Open Plan	From the current unit folder.
Save the document as **My plan**	In the current unit folder.
2 Select **Outlander Spices**	(In the first line on page 1.) You'll apply a style to this text.
3 Click ![44]	(The Styles and Formatting button is on the Formatting toolbar.) To display the Styles and Formatting task pane. This pane displays the current formatting of the selected text and lists the available styles.
4 From the Pick formatting to apply list, select **Heading 1**	
Deselect the text	
	The font size and style of the text have changed.
5 Update the document	

Creating styles by example

Explanation

You can use the Format Painter tool to copy the formatting from one text selection to another. However, if you plan to use the same formatting properties repeatedly, it's more efficient to create a new style based on the formatting of selected text.

To do this:

1. Select the text on which you want to base the new style.
2. On the Formatting toolbar, click anywhere in the Style list to select it.
3. Type a name for the new style.
4. Press Enter to create the style, which will now be available in the Style list.

Do it!

A-2: Creating a style by example

Here's how	Here's why
1 Select **The project team**	You'll create a style based on the formatting of this text.
2 On the Formatting toolbar, select the Style box	**4 pt, Bold, Italic** ▾
	(Click in the Style list box to select its contents.) You'll enter a name for the new style by editing this text.
In the Style list, enter **My subtitle**	**My subtitle** ▾
	This will be the name of the new style.
Press (↵ ENTER)	To create the style. The new style is also added to the task pane.
3 Select **Ann Salinski, VP Financial Services**	You'll apply the new style to this text.
From the Style list, select **My subtitle**	To apply the style to the selected text.
Deselect the text	
4 Update the document	

The Styles and Formatting task pane

Explanation

You can also use the Styles and Formatting task pane to create styles. You can either create a style from scratch or modify an existing style and save it with a new name.

To create a new style:

1 Display the Styles and Formatting pane.

2 Click New Style to open the New Style dialog box, as shown in Exhibit 4-2.

3 In the Name box, enter a name for the style.

4 From the Style type list, select one of the following types: Paragraph, Character, Table, or List.

5 From the Style based on list, select the style on which you want to base the new style.

6 Under Formatting, specify options such as font, tab settings, borders, and numbering.

7 Click OK to close the dialog box and to save the new style.

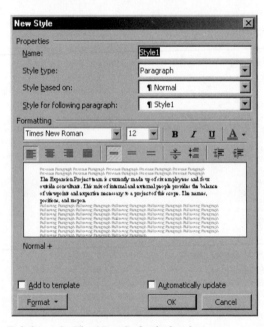

Exhibit 4-2: The New Style dialog box

Do it!

A-3: Using the Styles and Formatting task pane

Here's how	Here's why
1 In the task pane, click **New Style**	To open the New Style dialog box.
2 Under Properties, edit the Name box to read **My title**	To name the style you'll create.

3 From the Style based on list, select **Title**

The styles are listed in alphabetical order, so you'll need to scroll down to find the Title style. A sample of the selected style appears in the preview area.

4 Under Formatting, from the Font list, select **Courier New**

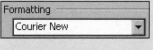

From the Size list, select **18**

Click I

To apply italics.

5 Observe the text below the preview area

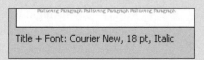

The details of the style are noted here. Title is listed first because the new style is based on the Title style; then the other formatting definitions are listed.

6 Click **OK**

Your new style (My title) and the style that it's based on (Title) appear in the Pick formatting to apply list.

7 Select **Outlander Spices**

You'll apply the new style to this text. In the task pane, in the Formatting of selected text box, the current style (Heading 1) appears.

In the task pane, point to **Heading 1**

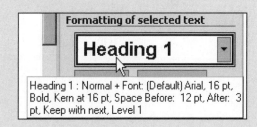

A ScreenTip lists the formatting details of the selected text.

8 From the Pick formatting to apply list, select **My title**

To apply the My title style to "Outlander Spices." The style name now appears at the top of the task pane in the Formatting of selected text box.

Deselect the text

9 Update the document

List styles

Explanation

Word's built-in styles include a variety of list styles. A list style can define formats (such as bullets or numbering) for several levels within a list. To apply a list style to selected text, use one of the following methods:

- On the Formatting toolbar, display the Style list, and select the required list style.
- In the Styles and Formatting task pane, select the required list style from the Pick formatting to apply list.
- In the Bullets and Numbering dialog box, click the List Styles tab, and select the required style.

Custom list styles

If none of the list styles suit your requirements, you can create a new list style. For example, you might want to display the first-level text in a different color. The Add to template option saves the new style to the template on which the document is based. Then, whenever you work in a document based on that template, your custom list style will be available.

To create a list style:

1 Display the Styles and Formatting task pane.
2 Click the New Style button.
3 In the Name box, enter a name for the list style.
4 From the Style type list, select List.
5 Specify the formatting properties for each level. By default, 1st level is selected.
6 Click OK to save the new list style.

Do it!

A-4:   Defining and applying a list style

Here's how	Here's why
1 Open Products	This document contains a list of products. The list has two levels: one for the category, and another for the products.
Save the document as **My products**	In the current unit folder.
2 Display the Styles and Formatting task pane	If necessary, click the Styles and Formatting button on the Formatting toolbar.
3 Open the New Style dialog box	Click New Style in the task pane.
4 Under Properties, edit the Name box to read **My list**	To specify a name for the style.
From the Style type list, select **List**	

5 Under Formatting, observe the
   Apply formatting to list

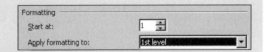

By default, 1st level is selected. You'll start by
setting the formatting options for the first level
of the list.

6 Click **B**

To set a bold style for the first level of the list.

   From the Number style list, select
   as shown

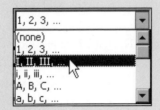

This change is reflected in the preview area of
the New Style dialog box.

7 From the Apply formatting to list,
   select **2nd level**

To begin setting the formatting options for the
second level of the list.

   From the Number style list, select
   the indicated bullet style

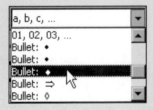

To apply a diamond shaped bullet to the second
level.

   Click **OK**

To close the dialog box and create the list style.

8 Select all the text in the document

(Choose Edit, Select All, or press Ctrl+A.)
You'll apply the new list style to the document
text.

   Apply the **My list** style

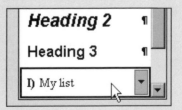

   Deselect the text

The product categories are now preceded by
Roman numerals, and the individual products
are listed with diamond-shaped bullets.

9 Update and close the document

Table styles

Explanation

You can define custom table styles and use them in documents. Table styles can also be added to the template on which a document is based. To apply a table style, use one of the following methods:

- On the Formatting toolbar, display the Style list, and select the required table style.
- In the Styles and Formatting task pane, select the required table style from the Pick formatting to apply list.
- In the Bullets and Numbering dialog box, click the List Styles tab, and select the required style.

To create a table style by using the Styles and Formatting task pane:

1 Display the Styles and Formatting task pane.
2 Click the New Style button.
3 In the Name box, enter a name for the table style.
4 From the Style type list, select Table.
5 From the Style based on list, select the existing table format on which you want to base your new style.
6 From the Apply formatting to list, select the portion of the table to which you want to apply a format. By default, the entire table is selected.
7 Specify the formatting properties for the table.
8 Click OK to close the dialog box and to save the table style.

Do it!

A-5:   Defining and applying a table style

Here's how	Here's why
1 Open Sales	
Save the document as **My sales**	
2 In the Styles and Formatting task pane, click **New Style**	
3 Under Properties, edit the Name box to read **My table**	
4 From the Style type list, select **Table**	Name: My table / Style type: Paragraph / Style based on: / Style for following paragraph: / Paragraph / Character / Table / List
5 From the Style based on list, select **Table List 4**	Under Formatting, a preview of the table style appears. In the Apply formatting to list, Whole table is selected by default.

6 Click as shown

To display the text alignment options.

Click **Align Center**

The text will be centered both vertically and horizontally.

7 From the Apply formatting to list, select **Header row**

8 Click as shown

To display the font color palette.

Select **Dark Blue**

The header row text will appear in this color, as indicated in the preview area.

Click **OK**

To close the New Style dialog box and create the new table style.

9 Select the table

10 Apply the **My table** style

Use the Pick formatting to apply list in the task pane.

Deselect the table

Update and close the document

Topic B: Modifying and deleting styles

This topic covers the following Microsoft Office Specialist exam objective.

#	Objective
WW03S-3-1	Applying styles to and clearing styles from text, tables, and lists (This objective is also covered in Topic A.)

Modifying styles

Explanation

One of the advantages of using styles is the ease with which you can make global changes. For example, if you modify any of a style's properties, then all text formatted with that style automatically inherits the new properties. This can be a major time saver.

To modify a style, you use the Modify Style dialog box, shown in Exhibit 4-3. From here, you can change the style's font, paragraph, border, tab, and numbering formats. To modify a style:

1 Display the Styles and Formatting task pane.
2 In the Pick formatting to apply list, right-click the style you want to modify.
3 From the shortcut menu, choose Modify to open the Modify Style dialog box.
4 Use the Formatting buttons and lists to specify new formatting options.
5 Click OK to close the Modify Style dialog box and to save the new settings.

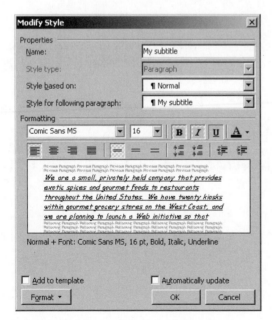

Exhibit 4-3: The Modify Style dialog box

Automatically updating styles

You can also redefine the style whenever manual formatting is applied to it. To do so, you need to check the Automatically update check box. For example, you might want to change the font color of the text after applying a specific style. This change will be reflected in the definition of the style only if you have checked the Automatically update check box.

Do it!

B-1: Modifying a style

Here's how	Here's why
1 Verify that My plan is open and no text is selected	
2 In the Pick formatting to apply list, point to **My subtitle**	To activate the down arrow.
Click the down-arrow as shown	 My subtitle Select All 1 Instance(s) Modify... Delete... Update to Match Selection To display the shortcut menu.
3 Choose **Modify...**	To open the Modify Style dialog box.
Under Formatting, from the Font list, select **Comic Sans MS**	To change the font to Comic Sans MS.
Change the font size to **16**	
Apply an underline	Your Modify Style dialog box should match the one shown in Exhibit 4-3.
4 Click **OK**	To close the Modify Style dialog box and view the changes in the document. The text "The project team" and "Ann Salinski, VP, Financial Services" has changed to reflect the modified style settings.
5 Update the document	

Overriding styles

Explanation

There might be times when you want to change the formatting of text after applying a style to it. For example, after applying the Heading 1 style, you might decide to increase the heading font to 20pt. You do this by selecting the text and applying the desired formatting. This action overrides the formatting contained in the style.

When you override a style, the Styles and Formatting task pane shows the additional formatting next to the style name, as shown in Exhibit 4-4. If you would prefer to see only styles in the Pick formatting to apply list, then display the Show list, and select Available styles.

Note: The automatic-update feature controls whether styles can be overridden. If you check the Automatically update check box when defining a style, then the action of adding manual formatting will modify, not override, the style.

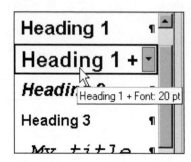

Exhibit 4-4: The Heading 1 style after you override the font size

Do it!

B-2: Overriding a style

Here's how	Here's why
1 Select **Outlander Spices**	You'll override the style applied to this text. In the Formatting of selected text box, My title appears.
2 Click U	(The Underline button is on the Formatting toolbar.) To override the My title style, applied earlier, by underlining the selected text. In the task pane, a new style entry called "My title + Underline" is added.
3 Change the font size to **24**	To override the My title style again. The changes are reflected in the Style list on the Formatting toolbar and in the Formatting of selected text box.
4 Point to the new formatting as shown	le + 24 pt, Un Normal My title + Font: 24 pt, Underline To see the ScreenTip, which displays the additional formatting you applied to the text.
5 From the Show list, select **Available styles**	Available formatting Formatting in use Available styles All styles Custom... Show: Available formatting To view only the available styles in the Pick formatting to apply list. My title + 24 pt, Underline is no longer displayed in the task pane because it wasn't saved as a style.
6 Update the document	

Deleting styles

Explanation

You can delete a style from a document by using the Styles and Formatting task pane. To do so, display the style shortcut menu and choose Delete. You will be prompted to confirm the deletion. When you delete a paragraph style, text that has been formatted with that style will revert to the Normal paragraph style.

Do it!

B-3: Deleting a style

Here's how	Here's why
1 In the Pick formatting to apply list, right-click **My title**	You can also click the down arrow next to the style name.
2 Choose **Delete...**	

> **Microsoft Word** ✕
>
> (?) Do you want to delete style My title?
>
> [Yes] [No]

A confirmation message box appears.

Click **Yes**	To delete the style. The text with the My title style applied, "Outlander Spices," has returned to Normal style. However, the manual formatting (24 pt. and underlined) is not removed along with the style.
3 Verify that the My title style is no longer available	Observe the Styles list on the Formatting toolbar, as well as the Pick formatting to apply list in the task pane.
4 Apply the **Heading 1** style to **Outlander Spices**	
5 Update the document	

Topic C: Navigating in large documents

This topic covers the following Microsoft Office Specialist exam objectives.

#	Objective
WW03S-1-3	Moving to selected content (e.g., Select Browse Object, Document Map) (This objective is also covered in *Word 2003: Basic*, in the unit titled "Editing documents.")
WW03S-2-2	Creating outlines
WW03S-5-7	Viewing reading layout, normal, outline, full screen, zoom views (This objective is also covered in *Word 2003: Basic*, in the units titled "Editing documents" and "Proofing and printing documents.")
WW03E-2-5	Using automation features for document navigation (e.g., Document Map, Thumbnails)

Outline view

Explanation

Word provides some helpful tools for navigating in long documents. Outline view enables you to collapse and expand text to view different levels.

When you format a document with heading styles, Word automatically creates an outline. You can use Outline view to see how the document is organized and to easily rearrange it. You can switch to Outline view by choosing View, Outline. Exhibit 4-5 shows a document in Outline view.

To prepare a document and display it in Outline view:

1 Apply Heading 1, Heading 2, and Heading 3 styles to headings and subheadings in a document.

2 Choose View, Outline. The Outlining toolbar appears.

3 Use the Show Level list to control how much of the outline is displayed. The default setting, Show All Levels, displays the entire document.

In Outline view, the plus sign (+) indicates that there is additional text under the level heading. You can use the Expand and Collapse buttons on the Outlining toolbar to display and hide selected portions of the document.

Exhibit 4-5: A document in Collapsed Outline view

Do it!   **C-1:   Creating a document outline**

Here's how	Here's why
1 Observe the style applied to Outlander Spices	The Heading 1 style is applied.
2 Select **The project team**	You'll apply the Heading 2 style to this text.
Apply the **Heading 2** style	From the Style list, select Heading 2.
Apply the **Heading 2** style to these headings: **Project Justification**, **Progress to date**, **Outstanding issues for Phase One**	
3 Apply the **Heading 3** style to **Ann Salinski, VP Financial Services**	
Apply the **Heading 3** style to the remaining names and titles	There are five more names: Jack Thomas, Elise Sechan, Aileen MacElvoy, Ron Timmons, and Kim Leong. At the end of this step, your outline will consist of three levels.
4 Press ⌈CTRL⌉ + ⌈HOME⌉	To go to the top of the document and deselect the text.
Choose **View**, **Outline**	To view the document structure. The Outlining toolbar appears. The entire document appears with text indented under headings. All headings are preceded by a plus (+) sign because they all have subtext.
5 From the Show Level list, select **Show Level 3**	
	(The Show Level list is on the Outlining toolbar.) You'll see the headings through the third level, as shown in Exhibit 4-5.
6 From the Show Level list, select **Show Level 2**	To view the headings from Level 1 ("Outlander Spices") and Level 2 ("The project team," "Project Justification," "Progress to date," and "Outstanding issues for Phase One").
Close the Styles and Formatting task pane	
7 Update the document	

The Document Map pane

Explanation

The Document Map feature displays document headings by level in a navigational pane, as shown in Exhibit 4-6. This view can be helpful when you need to work your way through a long document. Suppose you're working on a document with a first-level heading on each page. As you progress through each page, the corresponding heading in the Document Map pane is selected. For the Document Map pane to be used, the document must contain built-in heading styles.

By using this pane, you can selectively view the heading levels in a document. Each heading in a Document Map has an associated shortcut menu. You can choose options from this menu to view headings at different levels and to collapse or expand heading levels.

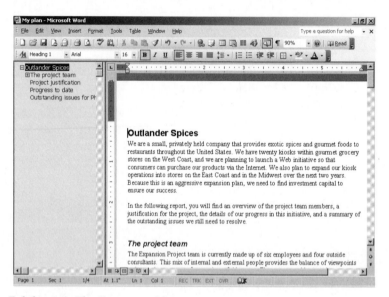

Exhibit 4-6: The Document Map pane

Do it!

C-2: Using the Document Map pane

Here's how	Here's why
1 Choose **View**, **Print Layout**	To switch to Print Layout view. The outline marks and the Outlining toolbar are no longer displayed.
2 Choose **View**, **Document Map**	To open the Document Map pane, as shown in Exhibit 4-6. This pane displays the levels of headings in the document. The minus (-) sign next to "Outlander Spices" indicates that all headings below it are displayed. The plus (+) sign next to "The project team" indicates that there are some headings hidden beneath this heading level. You'll selectively view and hide different heading levels and their associated details.

3 In the Document Map pane, select **The project team**

In the document, the insertion point moves to "The project team."

Click as shown

To expand the level "The project team" and display the Heading 3 level. The symbol to the left of "The project team" changes to a minus sign (-), which you can click to collapse the level.

4 In the Document Map pane, select **Kim Leong**

The document area now displays "Kim Leong" and his information. You can use the Document Map pane to navigate to other areas in the document.

5 Click as shown

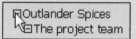

To collapse the heading levels displayed in the Document Map. The document area is unaffected.

6 Choose **View**, **Document Map**

To close the Document Map pane.

Update the document

Thumbnails

Explanation

Thumbnails are miniature images of the pages in a document. You can use thumbnails to easily navigate through a large document. Thumbnails appear on the left side of the Word window, as shown in Exhibit 4-7. The page numbers also appear to the left of the thumbnails.

You can view page thumbnails by choosing View, Thumbnails. To navigate to a specific page, click the thumbnail image of that page.

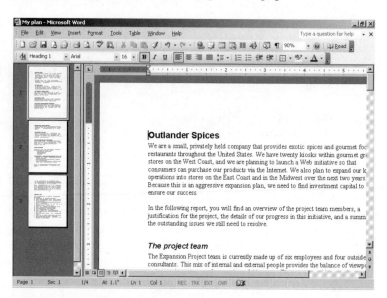

Exhibit 4-7: A sample document showing thumbnails

Do it!

C-3: Using thumbnails

Here's how	Here's why
1 Choose **View**, **Thumbnails**	The thumbnails of the document pages appear on the left side of the Word window, as shown in Exhibit 4-7.
2 Click on the thumbnail of the third page	The third page of the document appears on the right side of the window.
3 Choose **View**, **Thumbnails**	To return to Print Layout view.
4 Close the document	

Unit summary: Working with styles

Topic A   In this topic, you learned how to use **styles** to apply multiple formats at once. You created a new style by example. You also used the Styles and Formatting task pane to create a list style and a table style.

Topic B   In this topic, you learned how to **modify** and **delete styles** by using the Styles and Formatting task pane. You also learned how to **override a style's formatting** by manually changing the formatting of text.

Topic C   In this topic, you applied heading styles to create a document outline. You examined **Outline view** and used the Outlining toolbar to display the various levels of the outline. You also displayed and used the **Document Map** pane and **thumbnail** images to navigate in a large document.

Independent practice activity

1   Open Structure and save it as **My structure**.

2   Use the Style list to apply the Heading 2 style to the text "Zenith Garments Inc. Organizational structure."

3   Use the Styles and Formatting task pane to change the style of the same text to Heading 1.

4   Create a new style named **New heading** based on the Heading 2 style. The new style should have the following properties:
   - Font: Comic Sans MS
   - Font size: 16 point
   - Font color: Blue

5   Apply the New heading style to the word "Hierarchy."

6   Apply the Heading 2 style to the headings "President," "General Manager," "Vice Presidents," and "Regional Managers."

7   Apply the Heading 3 style to the subheadings "North and West regions," "South and East regions," "North region," "South region," and "East region."

8   Use Outline view to display the first three heading levels of the document.

9   Compare your work to Exhibit 4-8.

10   Close the Styles and Formatting task pane and the Outlining toolbar.

11   Update and close the document, but do not close Word.

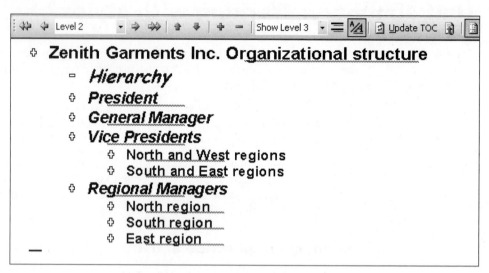

Exhibit 4-8: The document after Step 8 of the Independent Practice Activity

Review questions

1 What are some advantages of using styles?

2 What are the two ways to apply a style?

3 How do you create a style by example?

4 When creating a new list style, how can you make sure the style is available for other documents?

A Use the Format Painter tool

B Use the Add to template option

C Use the Styles and Formatting task pane

D Use the Save style tool

5 What are the different style types that you can create?

6 How do you access the Modify Style dialog box to redefine a style?

7 In the Styles and Formatting task pane, the Style shortcut menu can be used to do which of the following?

A Delete the style

B Modify the style

C Apply the style

D All of the above

8 What is a Document Map?

9 Which of the following prepares a document for Outline view?

A Applying heading styles

B Displaying the Outlining toolbar

C Opening the Styles and Formatting task pane

D Clicking the Outline view button

10 What is does the command View, Thumbnails do?

Unit 5

Headers and footers

Unit time: 30 minutes

Complete this unit, and you'll know how to:

A Create headers and footers for the first page, odd and even pages, and sections in a document.

B Insert and format page numbers and chapter numbers in a document.

Topic A: Different headers and footers

This topic covers the following Microsoft Office Specialist exam objective.

#	Objective
WW03S-3-4	Inserting and modifying content in document headers and footers (This objective is also covered in *Word 2003: Basic*, in the unit titled "Controlling page layout.")

First-page headers and footers

Explanation

Headers and footers are blocks of text that appear at the top and bottom of every page. Frequently, you'll want the header and footer on the first page of your document to be different from those that appear in the rest of the document. You can create unique first-page headers and footers by using the various options in the Layout tab of the Page Setup dialog box, as shown in Exhibit 5-1.

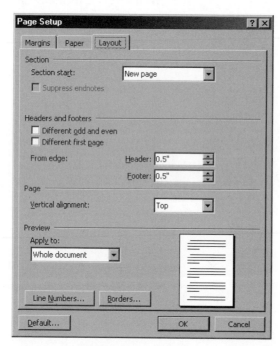

Exhibit 5-1: The Page Setup dialog box showing the Layout tab

To create a first-page header and footer:

1 Choose View, Header and Footer to display the Header and Footer area and toolbar.

2 Click the Page Setup button on the Header and Footer toolbar to display the Page Setup dialog box. Click the Layout tab, if necessary.

3 On the Layout tab, under Headers and Footers, check the Different first page box.

4 Click OK.

5 In the header area, enter text for the header.

6 In the footer area, enter text for the footer.

7 Close the Header and Footer toolbar.

Do it!

A-1: Creating a first-page header and footer

Here's how	Here's why
1 Open Progress	(From the current unit folder.) You'll learn how to control page layout by using the different tabs in the Page Setup dialog box.
Save the document as **My progress**	
2 Choose **View**, **Header and Footer**	(The Header and Footer toolbar appears.) The header area is identified by the word "Header."
3 Click 📖	(The Page Setup button is on the Header and Footer toolbar.) To open the Page Setup dialog box.
Click the **Layout** tab	If necessary.
Under Headers and footers, check **Different first page**	 Headers and footers ☐ Different odd and even ☑ Different first page To specify that the document will have a separate header for the first page.
Click **OK**	To apply the new settings and close the Page Setup dialog box.
4 Place the insertion point in the First Page Header area	First Page Header (If necessary.) The header area is now labeled First Page Header.
Type **Phase One Report**	
5 Click ▤	(The Switch Between Header and Footer button is on the Header and Footer toolbar.) To switch to the first-page footer.
In the footer area, type **Page**	To enter the text for the footer.
Press (SPACEBAR)	
Click 🔢	The Insert Page Number button is on the Header and Footer toolbar.
Click ≡	(The Center button is on the Formatting toolbar.) To center the footer.

6 Click **Close**
(The Close button is on the Header and Footer toolbar.) To save your changes and close the Header and Footer toolbar.

7 Choose **File**, **Print Preview**
To view the document with the header and footer.

From the Zoom list, select **100%**

You'll see "Phase One Report" in the first-page header and "Page 1" in the first-page footer. You'll add different header and footer text for the remaining pages.

8 Click **Close**
(The Close button is on the Print Preview toolbar.) To return to Normal view.

9 Update the document

Headers and footers for odd and even pages

Explanation

You can create different headers and footers for odd and even pages by checking the Different odd and even option on the Layout tab of the Page Setup dialog box. The header areas are identified as "Even Page Header" and "Odd Page Header." The same is true for the footer area. The different odd and even headers and footers are applied to the entire document. However, if you also check the Different first page box, then that setting will control the first-page header and footer.

Do it!

A-2: Creating odd- and even-page headers and footers

Here's how	Here's why
1 Display the Header and Footer toolbar	Choose View, Header and Footer.
2 Open the Page Setup dialog box	Click the Page Setup button on the Header and Footer toolbar.
3 Under Headers and footers, check **Different odd and even**	Headers and footers ☑ Different odd and even ☑ Different first page
Click **OK**	To apply the new settings.
4 Click in the Even Page Header area	You'll specify a header for the even page.
Type **Progress Report**	Even Page Header Progress Report
5 Click 🖹	(The Show Next button is on the Header and Footer toolbar.) To move to the odd-page header.
6 Type **Created on**	
Press (SPACEBAR)	
Click 📅	Odd Page Header Created on 7/29/2003
	(The Insert Date button is on the Header and Footer toolbar.) To insert the current date in the odd-page header.
7 Click ▤	(The Align Right button is on the Formatting toolbar.) To right-align the odd-page header.

8	Switch to the footer area	You'll specify a footer for the odd page.
	In the Odd Page Footer area, type **Page**	
	Press (SPACEBAR)	
	Click [#]	The Insert Page Number button is on the Header and Footer toolbar.
	Right-align the footer	Click the Align Right button on the Formatting toolbar.
9	Click [▣]	(The Show Previous button is on the Header and Footer toolbar.) To move to the previous page footer, which is an even-page footer.
10	Type **Page** as the footer text, and insert the page number	_ Even Page Footer_ Page 2
	Click **Close**	To close the Header and Footer toolbar.
11	Switch to Print Layout view	
	Scroll through the document	To view the headers and footers you just created.
12	Update the document	

Headers and footers for different document sections

Explanation

You might need to add headers and footers for different sections in a document. You can do this by inserting section breaks. When you create a new section, Word uses the previous section's header as the header of the new section. Before you can create new headers and footers for the section, you need to remove the link to the previous header and footer. To do so, display the Header and Footer toolbar, and click the Link to Previous button.

Do it!

A-3: Creating section headers and footers

Here's how	Here's why
1 On page 3, insert a Next page section break before "Progress to date"	(Choose Insert, Break; under Section break types, select Next page.) To divide the document into two sections. You'll create a different header and footer for this section.
2 Display the Header and Footer toolbar	First Page Header -Section 2- .... Same as Previous / Phase One report
	"First Page Header -Section2-" appears above the header area. The headers and footers from the previous section appear in the new section.
3 Click 🔲	(The Link to Previous button is on the Header and Footer toolbar.) To remove the link because you want to create a new header for the new section.
Edit the section header to read **Progress to date**	To change the header.
4 Switch to the footer area	As specified, the page number for this section is the next sequential number.
Click 🔲	To remove the link to the previous footer.
Left-align the footer	
5 Close the Header and Footer toolbar	You can scroll to see that this section's header is different from the other headers in the document.
6 Update and close the document	

Topic B: Page numbering

This topic covers the following Microsoft Office Specialist exam objective.

#	Objective
WW03S-3-4	Inserting and formatting page numbers

The Page Numbers dialog box

Explanation

Although the Header and Footer toolbar can be used to add page numbers to a document, you are limited to simple page numbers. You can use the Page Numbers dialog box to apply other types of page numbers, such as Roman numerals or chapter numbers.

The Insert, Page Numbers command opens the Page Numbers dialog box, shown in Exhibit 5-2. You can use this dialog box to specify the page number's position and alignment. You can also choose to suppress the number on the first page.

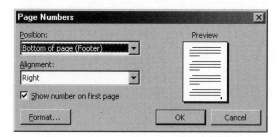

Exhibit 5-2: The Page Numbers dialog box

Do it!

B-1: Inserting page numbers

Here's how	Here's why
1 Open Outlander	You'll insert page numbers in this three-page document.
Save the document as **My outlander**	
2 Choose **Insert**, **Page Numbers…**	To open the Page Numbers dialog box. In the Position list, Bottom of page (Footer) is the default setting. The Show number on first page option is checked.
From the Alignment list, select **Center**	
Click **OK**	To insert the page number at the center of the page.
3 Scroll down to view the page numbers	The page numbers are in the center of the footer on each page of the document.
4 Update the document	

Suppressing numbering for the first page

If the first page of a document is a title page, it doesn't need to be numbered. You can suppress the page number on the first page by clearing the Show number on first page option in the Page Numbers dialog box.

B-2:   Suppressing the page number for the first page

Here's how	Here's why
1 Move to the first page of the document	If necessary.
2 Open the Page Numbers dialog box	Choose Insert, Page Numbers.
Clear **Show number on first page**	 To suppress the page number on the first page.
Click **OK**	The page number has been removed from only the first page.
3 Update the document	

Formatting page numbers

Explanation

In addition to specifying the position and alignment of page numbers, you can specify a number format, such as Arabic numbers, Roman numerals, or letters. You can also include chapter numbers with the page numbers. To access the formatting options, click the Format button in the Page Numbers dialog box.

The following table describes the components of the Page Number Format dialog box:

Component	Description
Number format	Select different numbering formats, such as Arabic numbers, Roman numerals, or letters of the alphabet.
Include chapter number	Select the heading style that identifies the start of a new chapter and the separator to be used.
Page numbering	Select continuous numbering, or enter a specific starting number.

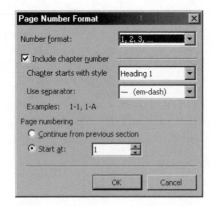

Exhibit 5-3: The Page Number Format dialog box

Do it! **B-3:   Formatting page numbers**

Here's how	Here's why
1 Open the Page Numbers dialog box	
2 Click **Format**	To open the Page Number Format dialog box, shown in Exhibit 5-3.
3 From the Number format list, select Roman numerals	Number format: [I, II, III, ... ▼]
Clear **Include chapter number**	[☐ Include chapter number]

By default, the Include chapter number option is checked. Because your document doesn't have chapters, you can clear this option. |
Click **OK**	To close the Page Number Format dialog box.
4 Click **OK**	The page numbers now appear in Roman numerals centered at the bottom of the page. The first page is not numbered.
5 Update the document	

Page numbers for chapters

Explanation

When a document contains multiple chapters, you can precede the page number with the chapter number. For example, the page number for page 2 of Chapter 1 can be displayed as "1-2."

To use the chapter-numbering format, you must first apply a multilevel list, or outline, style to the document. Then, you can link the heading style to the outline level. You'll be prompted to do so if Word is unable to identify chapter numbers.

To prepare a document to use chapter numbers:

1 Choose Format, Bullets and Numbering, and activate the Outline Numbered tab.

2 Click Customize. If necessary, select any outline style to activate the button.

3 Under the Number format, set Level to 1.

4 Verify that the Number style and Start at box contain the desired settings.

5 Click More to display additional options.

6 From the Link level to style list, select Heading 1.

7 Click OK.

To add chapter numbers:

1 Choose Insert, Page numbers to open the Page Numbers dialog box.

2 Click Format.

3 Check the Include chapter number box.

4 From the Chapter starts with style list, select Heading 1.

5 Select a separator character. The em dash (—) is selected by default.

6 Click OK to close the Page Number Format dialog box.

7 Click OK to close the Page Numbers dialog box.

Do it!

B-4:   Including chapter numbers

Here's how	Here's why
1 Place the insertion point at the beginning of the document	If necessary.
2 Choose **Format**, **Bullets and Numbering...**	To open the Bullets and Numbering dialog box.
3 Click the **Outline Numbered** tab	
4 Select the second number format, as shown	The Customize button becomes active when you select a format.
5 Click **Customize**	To open the Customize Outline Numbered List dialog box.
6 Under Number format, verify that Level 1 is selected	You'll apply the formatting to only the first level text.
In the Number style list, verify that 1, 2, 3, ... appears	
In the Start at box, verify that 1 appears	
7 Click **More**	To display more options at the bottom of the dialog box.
From the Link level to style list, select **Heading 1**	
Click **OK**	To close the Customize Outline Numbered List dialog box. You'll see that the text in Heading 1 style is numbered.

8	Open the Page Number Format dialog box	Choose Insert, Page Numbers, and click Format.
	Check **Include chapter number**	
	Under Include chapter number, verify that the options shown appear	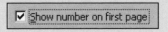
	From the Number format list, select **1, 2, 3, ...**	
	Click **OK**	To close the Page Number Format dialog box.
9	Check **Show number on first page**	☑ Show number on first page
		To number the first page.
	Click **OK**	
10	On page 3, insert a Next page section break before "Chapter 2: Our Products"	To move Chapter 2 to the next page.
	Click ¶	To display nonprinting characters.
	Scroll down to view the page number	The page numbering is wrong because a hard page break already existed between pages 2 and 3.
	Delete the hard page break	(Select the page break and press Delete.) At the bottom of page 2. The page numbering is now correct.
11	Hide nonprinting characters	
12	Update and close the document	

Unit summary: Headers and footers

Topic A   In this topic, you learned how to create a **unique header and footer** for the first page. You also created different headers and footers for odd and even pages and for sections.

Topic B   In this topic, you learned that the Insert, Page Numbers command can be used to insert page numbers of different styles. You used the **Page Number Format** dialog box to suppress page numbering for the first page. You also applied an outline style to a document so you could then include **chapter numbers** in the page numbers.

Independent practice activity

1 Open Celebrate, and save it as **My celebrate**.

2 For all pages except the first page, create a header saying **Outlander Spices**.

3 Create footers saying **Page 2 of 3** for the second page and **Page 3 of 3** for the third page.

4 Update and close the document.

5 Open Spices, and save it as **My spices**.

6 Insert page numbers in the document.

7 Suppress the first page's page number.

8 Apply a number format of your choice to the page numbers.

9 Update and close the document.

Review questions

1 Why are headers and footers usually suppressed on the first page of documents?

2 How do you create unique first-page headers and footers?

3 Name two ways to verify that the header and footer is correct.

4 Which of the following is true?

A You can create a unique header for a section.

B You can create a unique header for the first page.

C You can create a unique header for even pages.

D All of the above

5 Why would you insert a page number using the Page Numbers dialog box instead of the Header and Footer toolbar?

6 In the Page Number Format dialog box, which component enables you to enter a specific starting number?

A Number format

B Page numbering

C Include Chapter number

D Page Setup

7 Before chapter numbers can be added to pages, what must you do to the document?

Unit 6

Printing labels and envelopes

Unit time: 25 minutes

Complete this unit, and you'll know how to:

A Set up and print single labels and envelopes.

Topic A: Labels and envelopes

This topic covers the following Microsoft Office Specialist exam objective.

#	Objective
WW03S-5-5	Printing documents, envelopes, and labels (This objective is also covered in *Word 2003: Basic*, in the unit titled "Proofing and printing documents.")

Labels

Explanation

You can use the Envelopes and Labels dialog box to create and print labels and envelopes. This dialog box takes names and addresses from your address book or from a document and prepares labels or envelopes. After creating addresses for labels or envelopes, you can print them by clicking the Print button on the Envelopes and Labels dialog box.

You can print labels by using the Envelopes and Labels dialog box. To do so:

1 Choose Tools, Letters and Mailings, Envelopes and Labels.
2 Click the Labels tab to display the label options, as shown in Exhibit 6-1.
3 Specify the address in the Address box. To retrieve an address from your address book, click the Address Book button.
4 Use the Options button to specify the printer and label information.
5 In the Print area, select to print a full page of labels or just a single label.
6 Click Print to send the labels to the printer.

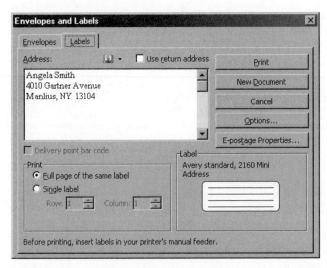

Exhibit 6-1: The Labels tab of the Envelopes and Labels dialog box

Do it!

A-1: Printing a single label

Here's how	Here's why
1 Open Address	This document contains a list of names and addresses. You'll print a label for the first address.
Save the document as **My address**	
2 Choose **Tools**, **Letters and Mailings**, **Envelopes and Labels...**	To open the Envelopes and Labels dialog box.
3 Click the **Labels** tab	In the Address box, the first address appears because the insertion point is there.
4 Under Print, select **Single label**	

Print
- ○ Full page of the same label
- ● Single label
  - Row: 1 Column: 1

To print a single mailing label.

5 Click **Options**	To open the Label Options dialog box. You can change the printer settings in this dialog box.
6 From the Label products list, select **Avery standard**	If necessary.
7 From the Product number list, select **3612 – Business Card**	

Label information

Type:	Business Card
Height:	2"
Width:	3.5"
Page size:	Letter (8 ½ x 11 in)

The information about the selected label type appears in the Label information box.

Click **OK**	To close the Label Options dialog box.
8 Click **Print**	To print the business card label.

Envelopes

Explanation

You can print single envelopes by using the Envelope tab in the Envelopes and Labels dialog box. As shown in Exhibit 6-2, you can specify both the delivery and return addresses. You can also attach the envelope to the document by clicking the Add to Document button.

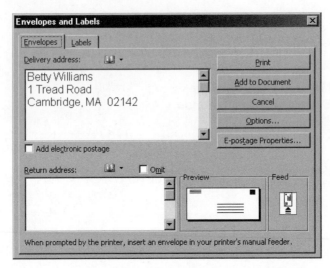

Exhibit 6-2: The Envelopes tab of the Envelopes and Labels dialog box

Do it!

A-2:   Printing a single envelope

Here's how	Here's why
1 Place the insertion point before the second address	You'll print this address on the envelope.
2 Open the Envelopes and Labels dialog box	Choose Tools, Letters and Mailings, Envelopes and Labels.
3 Click the **Envelopes** tab	To specify an address for the envelope. In the Delivery address box, the second address appears, as shown in Exhibit 6-2.
4 Check **Omit**	So that a return address is not printed on the envelope.
5 Click **Options**	To open the Envelope Options dialog box. By default, the standard business size 10 envelope is selected. A printed bar code can be added if you are mailing in the U.S. You can also change the delivery and return address fonts.
Click **OK**	To close the Envelope Options dialog box.
6 Click **Add to Document**

Betty Williams
1 Tread Road
Cambridge, MA 02142
———————— Section Break (Next Page) ————

Angela Smith
4010 Gartner Avenue
Manlius, NY 13104

The envelope is attached to the top of the document in a new section. Now, you can print the envelope by printing this page. |
| 7 Update and close the document | |

Unit summary: Printing labels and envelopes

Topic A In this topic, you learned how to print single **labels** and **envelopes** by using the Envelopes and Labels dialog box.

Independent practice activity

1 Create a new document with two addresses as shown in Exhibit 6-3.

2 Save the document as **My labels**.

3 Prepare to print one label by using Steve Paul's address. Cancel before printing unless you have a printer attached to your computer. From the Product number list, select 2162 Mini - Address.

4 Add an envelope to the document for Kate Thomas, as shown in Exhibit 6-4. You don't need a return address. Cancel before printing unless you have a printer attached to your computer.

5 Update and close the document.

```
Steve Paul
79 Oak Street
Chicago, IL 60610

Kate Thomas
58 Massachusetts Ave
Boston, MA 02210
```

Exhibit 6-3: The addresses to be entered in Step 1 of the Independent Practice Activity

```
                              Kate Thomas
                              58 Massachusetts Ave
                              Boston, MA 02210
                                        Section Break (Next Page)
Steve Paul
79 Oak Street
Chicago, IL 60610


Kate Thomas
58 Massachusetts Ave
Boston, MA 02210
```

Exhibit 6-4: The envelope after Step 4 of the Independent Practice Activity

Review questions

1 In the Envelopes and Labels dialog box, how do you specify a printer?

2 After creating a label, what are the two printing choices available?

3 What is the advantage to adding an envelope to the document?

4 True or False. A return address is required on envelopes.

5 How do you quickly create a label for an Outlook contact?

Unit 7

Working with graphics and objects

Unit time: 60 minutes

Complete this unit, and you'll know how to:

A Work with graphics and clip art.

B Insert WordArt and symbols into a document.

C Customize the background of a document.

D Use the Drawing tools to create objects.

Topic A: Working with graphics and clip art

This topic covers the following Microsoft Office Specialist exam objectives.

#	Objective
WW03S-1-4	Inserting, positioning and sizing graphics, text boxes and shapes (This objective is also covered in Topic D.)
WW03E-1-3	Wrapping text with graphics
WW03E-1-3	Cropping and rotating graphics (This objective is also covered in Topic D.)
WW03E-1-3	Controlling image contrast and brightness
WW03E-1-3	Scaling and resizing graphics
WW03E-1-4	Inserting and modifying new objects and objects from files (This objective is also covered in Topic B.)

Inserting graphics from files

Explanation

You can insert graphics either from image files or from the Clip Art Gallery that comes with Word. The Clip Art Gallery provides access to hundreds of professionally designed images.

If you have graphics that you would like to include in a document, you can use the Insert, Picture, From File command. To do this:

1 Choose Insert, Picture, From File to open the Insert Picture dialog box.

2 Navigate to the file you want to insert.

3 Click Insert.

Do it!

A-1: Inserting a graphic from a file

Here's how	Here's why
1 Open Chapter	From the current unit folder.
Save the document as **My chapter**	In the current unit folder.
2 Place the insertion point as shown	

|
Introduction

The buyers at Outlander Spices
vegetarian" products. Because

(If necessary.) You'll insert an image file.

| 3 Choose **Insert**, **Picture**, **From File...** | To open the Insert Picture dialog box. |

4 Navigate to the current unit folder

From the list, select **Title**

5 Click **Insert**

Outlander Spices

Adding spice to your life

Introduction

To insert the title image, Outlander Spices.

6 Update the document

Inserting clip art

Explanation

You can insert clip art into a document by using the Clip Art task pane. To do so:

1 Choose Insert, Picture, Clip Art, or click the Insert Clip Art button on the Drawing toolbar, to display the Clip Art task pane, shown in Exhibit 7-1.

2 Click the Go button on the task pane to display the available clips in the Results box.

3 Scroll through the Results box, and click the image you want to insert.

Exhibit 7-1: The Clip Art task pane

Do it!

A-2: Inserting clip art

Here's how	Here's why
1 Place the insertion point at the beginning of the first paragraph	You'll be inserting a clip art object here and then moving it to a new location.
2 Choose **View**, **Toolbars**, **Drawing**	To display the Drawing toolbar.
Click	(The Insert Clip Art button is on the Drawing toolbar.) To display the Clip Art task pane on the right side of the window.
3 In the Clip Art task pane, click **Go**	
	To see a preview of the available clips in the Results box. It might take a moment for the clips to appear. You can use the vertical scroll bar to view the clips.
4 Scroll down and click the cornucopia	
	The clip is inserted in the document.
5 In the Search for box, enter **Food**	
	To search for clips related to this topic.
Click **Go**	The Results box displays all clip art objects related to food. The clip art image you inserted in the document is also available.
6 Close the Clip Art task pane	
7 Update the document	

Modifying and moving graphics

Explanation

After inserting graphics, you can modify them in a variety of ways that include resizing, cropping, and moving them. You can use the Format Picture dialog box to perform many of these tasks.

Resizing graphics

To resize a graphic:

1 Choose Format, Picture to open the Format Picture dialog box.
2 Activate the Size tab, as shown in Exhibit 7-2.
3 In the Height and Width boxes, enter the desired values.
4 Click OK.

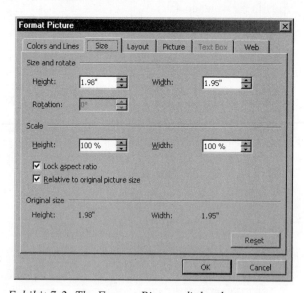

Exhibit 7-2: The Format Picture dialog box

You can also increase or decrease the size of a graphic by dragging one of the selection handles until the graphic reaches the size you want. Dragging the corner selection handles sizes the graphic proportionally.

Moving graphics

You can also move a graphic by using one of the following methods:

- Cut the graphic, and then paste it in the new location.
- Drag it to the new location. Avoid dragging the selection handles, or you will resize the graphic instead of moving it.

Cropping graphics

The process of cutting off a portion of a graphic is known as *cropping*. Unlike resizing, cropping changes the actual content of the graphic. Cropping can be used to remove extra white space around a graphic or to trim off a portion of a picture.

To crop a graphic:

1   Select the graphic to be cropped.

2   Click the Crop tool on the Picture toolbar. The crop symbol is added to the mouse pointer.

3   Drag the appropriate selection handle to crop, or trim, the object.

Do it!

A-3:   Modifying and moving a graphic

Here's how	Here's why
1 Select the cornucopia object	(If necessary.) When an object is selected, the object edges contain selection handles, and the Picture toolbar is displayed.
Choose **Format, Picture...**	To open the Format Picture dialog box.
2 Click the **Size** tab	To view the size and scale settings, as shown in Exhibit 7-2.
Under Scale, in the Height box, enter **75**	To change the height of the image.
Press (TAB)	To select the Width box and see that it changes automatically to 75 because Lock aspect ratio is checked.
Click **OK**	The size of the image is decreased to 75%.
3 Verify that the object is selected	
Point to the lower-right selection handle	
	The pointer takes the shape of a diagonal, two-headed arrow.
Drag the handle as shown	
	To proportionally decrease the size of the image.

4 Click [✄]

(The Cut button is on the Standard toolbar.) To cut the image.

5 On page 2, place the insertion point as shown

> **Dehydrated fruits and vegetables**
>
> Check out our Dried Fruits and Vegetables
> selection of dried beans, vegetables, and

At the beginning of the heading "Dehydrated fruits and vegetables."

Click [📋]

(The Paste button is on the Standard toolbar.) The image now appears at the new location.

6 Press (↵ ENTER)

To create a blank line.

7 Update the document

Contrast and brightness

Explanation

You might want to increase or decrease the contrast or brightness of a graphic in a document. To do so:

1 Select the image.

2 Choose Format, Picture to open the Format Picture dialog box. The Picture tab is activated by default.

3 Under Image control, enter the values that you want to use in the Contrast and Brightness boxes.

- The spinner control and scroll bars next to the specific options can also be used to change the setting.

- The four buttons on the Picture toolbar (More Contrast, Less Contrast, More Brightness, and Less Brightness) can also be used.

4 Click OK.

Do it!

A-4: Adjusting the contrast and brightness of a graphic

Here's how	Here's why
1 Select the object	
2 Choose **Format, Picture...**	To open the Format Picture dialog box. The Picture tab is activated by default.
3 In the Brightness box, enter **40**	To decrease the brightness of the image.
In the Contrast box, enter **75**	To increase the contrast.
Click **OK**	
	The image appears less bright, and the white drawing is emphasized more.
4 Update the document	

Borders

Explanation

You can add borders to images by using either the Border button on the Formatting toolbar or the Borders dialog box.

By default, borders are a solid black line that is 1/2 pt. wide. In the Borders dialog box, you can change the border style, width, and color.

Do it!

A-5: Adding a border to a graphic

Here's how	Here's why
1 Select the object	If necessary.
2 Right-click the selection	
From the shortcut menu, choose **Borders and Shading...**	To open the Borders dialog box so you can apply a box-type border to the object.
3 In the Borders tab, under Setting, select **Box**	
Click **OK**	To apply the default border around the selected object.
4 Deselect the image	

Dehydrated fruits and v
Check out our Dried Fruits
selection of dried beans, v

The border doesn't really match the graphic.

5 Select the image

Open the Borders dialog box

Right-click, and choose Borders and Shading.

From the Color list, select Light Orange

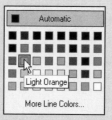

Change the width to **3/4 pt**

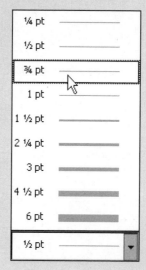

Click **OK**

6 Deselect the image

The border now matches the image and blends better.

7 Update the document

Text wrapping

Explanation

You can format the text around an object or picture in a number of ways. Using the Format Picture dialog box, you can align the object or picture with the text, behind the text, or in front of the text. To open this dialog box, select the object and choose Format, Picture. You can then select any wrapping style and horizontal alignment from the Layout tab.

You can wrap text around graphics by using the Advanced Layout dialog box, shown in Exhibit 7-3. To open this dialog box, click the Advanced button in the Format Picture dialog box.

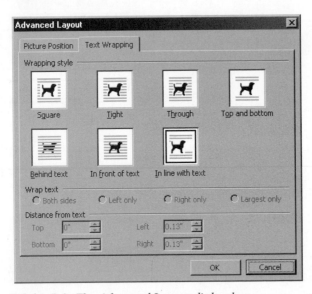

Exhibit 7-3: The Advanced Layout dialog box

Do it!

A-6: Wrapping text around a graphic

Here's how	Here's why
1 Select the object	
2 Right-click and choose **Format Picture...**	To use the shortcut menu to open the Format Picture dialog box.
Click the **Layout** tab	
Click **Advanced**	To open the Advanced Layout dialog box, shown in Exhibit 7-3.
3 Under Wrapping style, select **Tight**	
	This brings the text to the edges of the object.
Under Wrap text, select **Right only**	
	You'll align all the text to the right of the object.
Under Distance from text, in the Right box, enter **0.5"**	
Click **OK**	To close the Advanced Layout dialog box.
4 Click **OK**	To close the Format Picture dialog box. The image is on the left, and the text is placed to the right of the image.
5 Deselect the image	
6 Update the document	

Topic B: Inserting WordArt and symbols

This topic covers the following Microsoft Office Specialist exam objectives.

#	Objective
WW03S-1-1	Inserting text, symbols, hidden text and special characters (This objective is also covered in *Word 2003: Basic*, in the unit titled "Editing documents.")
WW03S-5-7	Splitting windows and arranging panes
WW03E-1-4	Inserting and modifying new objects and objects from files (This objective is also covered in Topic A.)

Inserting WordArt

Explanation

You can use WordArt to create special text effects, such as shadowing, skewing, or rotating text. The WordArt Gallery provides various styles for you to use. You can also insert symbols into documents by using the Symbol dialog box.

To insert WordArt objects into a document:

1 Click the Insert WordArt button on the Drawing toolbar, or choose Insert, Picture, WordArt, to display the WordArt Gallery dialog box, shown in Exhibit 7-4.

2 Select a style from the WordArt Gallery.

3 Click OK to open the Edit WordArt Text dialog box.

4 In the box, enter the text you want to insert.

5 Select the font and size you want to use.

6 Click OK to insert the text.

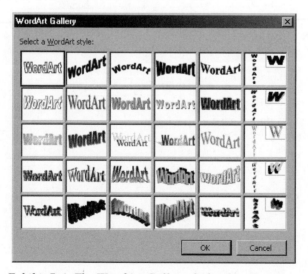

Exhibit 7-4: The WordArt Gallery dialog box

Do it!

B-1: Inserting a WordArt object

Here's how	Here's why
1 Place the insertion point before the heading **Introduction**	In the first page of the document.
Press (↵ ENTER)	To move the text to the next line.
Place the insertion point as shown	
2 Click [WordArt icon]	(The Insert WordArt button is on the Drawing toolbar.) To open the WordArt Gallery dialog box. You'll see a number of WordArt styles.
3 Select the indicated style	
Click **OK**

To close the WordArt Gallery dialog box. The Edit WordArt Text dialog box opens. |
| 4 Edit the Text box to read **Outlander Spices** | |
| From the Size list, select **24** | |
| Click **OK** |

To insert WordArt in the document. |
| 5 Update the document | |

Editing and moving WordArt objects

Explanation

After you insert a WordArt object into a document, you can modify the object to suit your needs. You can change the text or its formatting by using the Edit Text button on the WordArt toolbar or by choosing Edit Text from the shortcut menu.

As with other objects, you can move a WordArt object by using the following methods:

- Cut the object, and then paste it in the new location.
- Drag the object to the new location.

Splitting a window

When you are moving objects in a large document, you might find it helpful to split the window into two sections, or panes. This enables you to see two different parts of a large document at the same time. Use one of the following methods to split the window:

- Choose Window, Split. A shaded split bar appears with the two-headed resize arrow. Position the split bar in the desired location, and click the mouse. The window is now divided into two panes.
- Point to the Split box directly above the vertical scroll bar. Press and hold the mouse button as you drag the split bar to the desired location. When you release the mouse button, the window is divided into two panes.

You can remove the split by choosing Window, Remove Split. You can also remove the split by dragging the split bar off the page or by double-clicking it.

Exhibit 7-5: Using a split window to view two sections of a large document

Do it!

B-2:   Editing and moving a WordArt object

Here's how	Here's why
1 Select the WordArt object	The WordArt toolbar appears. Handles now appear around the text.
2 On the Word Art toolbar, click **Edit Text...**	The Edit WordArt Text dialog box opens.
3 From the Font list, select **Comic Sans MS**	To change the font of the inserted text.
Click **OK**	To apply the new font.
4 Deselect the WordArt	

Outlander Spices

The font of the text has changed.

5 Choose **Window**, **Split**	The shaded split bar appears across the window. The two-headed resize arrow is attached to the split bar.
Near the middle of the window, click the mouse	To split the window into top and bottom panes.
6 In the bottom pane, scroll to view page 3	One of the advantages of splitting windows is the ability to simultaneously view different areas of a large document.
Verify that you can see the "Online shopping" text	Your screen should resemble the window shown in Exhibit 7-5.
7 In the top pane, select the WordArt object	You'll move the WordArt to page 3.
Drag the object down to the blank line above "Online shopping"	

Outlander Spices

Online shopping
With our online shopping service, you can order

The Word Art object has moved from page 1 to page 3.

8 Choose **Window**, **Remove Split**	To return to a single window.
9 Update the document	

Symbols

Explanation You can insert symbols and special characters by using the Symbol dialog box, shown in Exhibit 7-6. To open the Symbol dialog box, choose Insert, Symbol. You can also assign keyboard shortcuts to the symbols you use frequently.

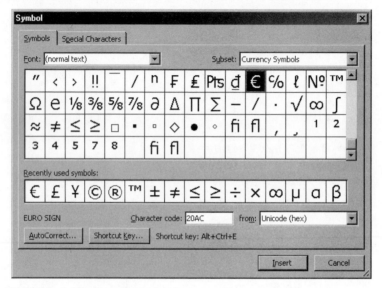

Exhibit 7-6: The Symbol dialog box

Do it!   **B-3:   Inserting a symbol**

Here's how	Here's why
1 Place the insertion point in the first paragraph, as shown	**Introduction** The buyers at Outlander Spices pride You'll insert a symbol here.
2 Choose **Insert**, **Symbol...**	To open the Symbol dialog box, shown in Exhibit 7-6. The Symbols tab is activated.
From the Font list, select **Symbol**	
3 Select the Registered symbol, as shown	
Click **Insert**	To insert the symbol in the document.
Click **Close**	To close the Symbol dialog box.
4 Observe the inserted symbol	**Outlander Spices®** The symbol has been inserted after the text.
5 Update and close the document	

Topic C: Customizing the background

This topic covers the following Microsoft Office Specialist exam objectives.

#	Objective
WW03E-3-2	Creating watermarks
WW03E-3-2	Applying themes
WW03E-3-2	Creating and modifying document background colors and fill effects

Background colors and fill effects

Explanation

You can customize the background of a document by using background colors and fill effects, watermarks, or themes. *Watermarks* refer to any text or image that can be seen behind the text in a document. For example, an organization's letterhead might have the company logo as a watermark. *Themes* contain styles and background colors that you can use for a consistent look among your documents.

Background colors can make documents more appealing. You can also apply special effects to the background. To do this, use the tabs in the Fill Effects dialog box. These tabs are:

- **Gradient** — Used to apply more than one color as a background and to apply various shading styles.
- **Texture** — Used to select the texture style with which the color can be filled.
- **Pattern** — Used to select the pattern—such as dotted, line, or bars—that the background color can appear in.
- **Picture** — Used to apply a picture as the background.

To apply background colors and fill effects to a document:

1 Choose Format, Background. Select a color to apply a solid background color.
2 Choose Format, Background, Fill Effects to open the Fill Effects dialog box, shown in Exhibit 7-7.
3 Use the Gradient, Texture, Pattern, and Picture tabs to specify the desired effects.
4 Click OK.

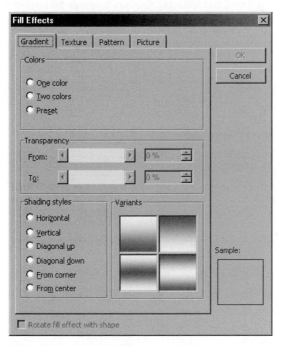

Exhibit 7-7: The Fill Effects dialog box

Do it!

C-1: Adding background colors and fill effects

Here's how	Here's why
1 Open Graphic	From the current unit folder.
Save the document as **My graphic**	In the current unit folder.
2 Choose **Format**, **Background**	
Choose the Light Green color	

	To apply light green as the background color of the document.
3 Choose **Format**, **Background**, **Fill Effects...**	To open the Fill Effects dialog box.
Under Colors, select **One color**	
Under Shading styles, select **From center**	

	To apply shading from the center to the corners of the page. A sample of the shading appears under Sample.
Click **OK**	To close the Fill Effects dialog box and apply the selected shading style.
4 Scroll through the document	To view the shading effect applied to the background.

5 Open the Fill Effects dialog box   Choose Format, Background, Fill Effects.

   Click the **Texture** tab

   Select the Parchment option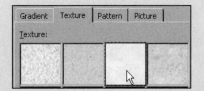

   Click **OK**   To apply a background texture that resembles parchment paper.

6 Update and close the document

Watermarks

Explanation

You can add text or a picture as a document's watermark. To add a text watermark:

1 Choose Format, Background, Printed Watermark to open the Printed Watermark dialog box.

2 Select Text watermark.

3 Select the text for the watermark. You can also add your own text.

4 Format the text by using the Font, Size, and Color lists.

5 Click Apply and then click OK.

To add a picture watermark, select the Picture watermark option in the Printed Watermark dialog box.

Do it!

C-2: Adding a watermark

Here's how	Here's why
1 Open Introduction	From the current unit folder.
Save the document as **My introduction**	In the current unit folder.
2 Choose **Format, Background, Printed Watermark...**	To open the Printed Watermark dialog box.
3 Select **Text watermark**	 The text and font options are now available.
4 From the Text list, select **SAMPLE**	To specify Sample as the text that will appear in the background of the document.
From the Font list, select **Arial Black**	To change the font. You can also specify a size for the text; however, we'll accept the Auto default setting.
Click **Apply**	
5 Click **Close**	The SAMPLE watermark appears diagonally behind the text.
6 Update the document	

Themes

Explanation

A *theme* is a named set of background and foreground images, formats, and styles that is applied to all pages in a document. When you apply a theme to a document, all the other formatting of the pages is removed, and the elements—such as background colors or graphics, heading styles, bullet lists, horizontal lines, hyperlink colors, and table border colors—are customized based on the theme.

To apply a theme:

1 Choose Format, Theme to open the Theme dialog box.

2 Under Choose a Theme, select a theme. Under Sample of theme, you can preview the theme.

3 Click OK.

Do it!

C-3:   Applying themes

Here's how	Here's why
1 Choose **Format, Theme...**	To open the Theme dialog box.
2 Under Choose a Theme, select **Blends**	
	You'll apply this theme to the document. You can see the preview of this theme in the Sample box.
Click **OK**	The background of the document changes. The font size also changes.
3 Click anywhere in the first paragraph	
Click ▤	
	To apply the bullet formatting to this paragraph and see what the bullets for this theme look like.
Click ▤ again	To remove the bullet formatting.
4 Update and close the document	

Topic D: Using drawing tools

This topic covers the following Microsoft Office Specialist exam objectives.

#	Objective
WW03S-1-4	Inserting, positioning and sizing graphics, text boxes and shapes (This objective is also covered in Topic A.)
WW03S-1-5	Creating and modifying charts and diagrams (This objective is also covered in the unit titled "Working with Excel data.")
WW03E-1-3	Cropping and rotating graphics (This objective is also covered in Topic A.)

The Drawing toolbar

Explanation

You can add drawing objects—such as squares, rectangles, curves, or lines—to documents. To do this, you can use the different options on the Drawing toolbar. When you're working with multiple objects, it can be helpful to group them together so you can work with them as one object.

To draw lines and figures by using the Drawing toolbar:

1 Choose View, Toolbars, Drawing to display the Drawing toolbar.
2 Click the line or shape you want to draw.
3 Drag to draw the line or shape.

When you start to draw a shape, the drawing canvas opens, as shown in Exhibit 7-8. The *drawing canvas* provides space where you can work on your drawing. The drawing canvas also contains the Drawing Canvas toolbar that provides tools you can use to resize, scale, or rotate drawings.

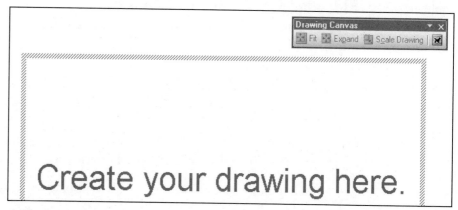

Exhibit 7-8: The drawing canvas with the Drawing Canvas toolbar

Rotating objects

The *Rotate handle* is the green circle that appears near the top of the selected object. You can use this handle to turn the object on an imaginary axis. To rotate an object:

1 Point to the Rotate handle to see that the mouse pointer changes.

2 Drag the Rotate handle until you reach the desired position. A dotted outline indicates how the object will be turned.

3 Release the mouse button to complete the rotation.

Do it!

D-1:   Creating lines and figures

Here's how	Here's why
1 Open a new document	
Save the document as **My drawing**	
2 Click [⬭]	(The Oval button is on the Drawing toolbar.) To draw an oval. The drawing canvas opens with the Drawing Canvas toolbar displayed, as shown in Exhibit 7-8.
3 Click in the center of the canvas	A circle appears in the canvas.
4 Drag the lower-left selection handle as shown	

To resize the circle as an oval.

| 5 Point to the green Rotate handle, as shown | |

The shape of the pointer changes when it's on the Rotate handle. Use the green Rotate handle to turn the drawings around.

| Drag right, as shown | |

The oval is rotated according to the position of the pointer.

| Restore the oval as shown, and deselect it | |

The rotate handle and the resizing handles disappear.

6 Click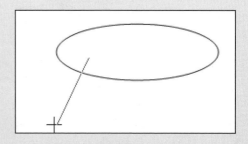

(The Line button is on the Drawing toolbar.)
You'll draw a line.

Click near the left side of the oval,
and drag as shown

To draw a line from the oval to the lower-left
region of the document.

Deselect the line

7 Click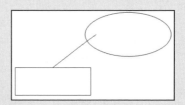

(The Rectangle button is on the Drawing
toolbar.) To draw a rectangle.

Draw a rectangle as shown

8 Draw another line and another
rectangle, as shown

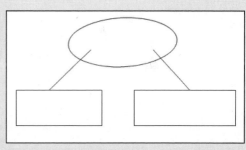

9 On the Drawing Canvas toolbar,
click **Expand**

To increase the size of only the drawing canvas
and not of the objects. You can enlarge the
drawing canvas further by continuing to click or
by dragging the sizing handles on the edge of
the canvas.

Click **Scale Drawing**

(On the Drawing Canvas toolbar.) The drawing
canvas frame changes, and the resizing handles
of the canvas become circles. When this button
is activated, both the objects and the drawing
canvas will be resized proportionally to each
other.

10 Decrease the size of the drawing canvas by dragging the middle-left resizing handle, as shown	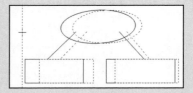
	The size of the object decreases along with the size of the drawing canvas. The shape of the pointer changes to a cross when the Scale Drawing button is activated.
11 On the Drawing Canvas toolbar, click **Fit**	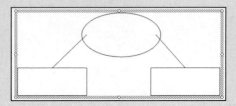
	To make the drawing canvas closely fit the size of the object.
Increase the size of the drawing canvas	Click the Expand button repeatedly or use the resizing handle after disabling the Scale Drawing button on the Drawing Canvas toolbar.
12 Update the document	

Grouping objects

Explanation

Grouping involves merging two or more drawing objects into a single unit. After grouping several drawing objects together, you can work with them as you would a single object. This helps you maintain the placement of the individual objects as you rotate, move, and flip the grouped object.

To group objects:

1 Select the first object you want to group.
2 Press and hold the Shift key as you click to select each additional object.
3 When all objects are selected, you can choose Draw, Group on the Drawing toolbar.

Do it!

D-2:   Grouping drawing objects

Here's how	Here's why
1 Press and hold ⟨ SHIFT ⟩	You'll select the oval, lines, and rectangles.
Select all of the drawn objects as shown	
Release ⟨ SHIFT ⟩	
2 Right-click the selected objects	To display a shortcut menu.
Choose **Grouping, Group**	
	To group the five objects as one.
3 Observe the figure	
	The five objects have been grouped into a single unit. The resizing handles are common for the group, and there is only one rotate handle.
4 Use the rotate handle to rotate the object	
	To rotate the entire group.
5 Undo the rotation	Press Ctrl+Z.
Deselect the group	
6 Update the document	

Text boxes

Explanation

You can enter text inside drawn objects by using a *text box*. To create a text box, click the Text Box button on the Drawing toolbar, and then click the location where you want to place the text box.

If the text doesn't fit well, you can resize the text box by dragging any of its selection handles. You can also modify a text box by using the Format Text Box dialog box, shown in Exhibit 7-9. To open the Format Text Box dialog box, select the text box you want to modify and choose Format, Text Box, or double-click the border of a text box.

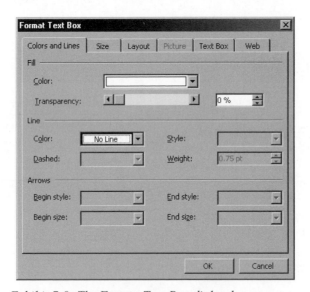

Exhibit 7-9: The Format Text Box dialog box

Do it!

D-3: Creating and modifying a text box

Here's how	Here's why
1 Click 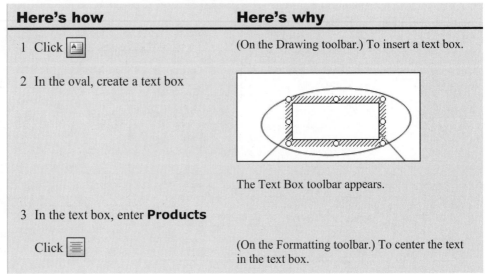	(On the Drawing toolbar.) To insert a text box.
2 In the oval, create a text box	The Text Box toolbar appears.
3 In the text box, enter **Products**	
Click	(On the Formatting toolbar.) To center the text in the text box.

4 Create two more text boxes, then enter and center the text in each box as shown

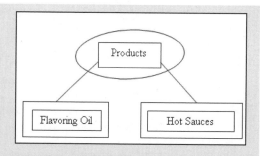

5 Select the Products text box   We don't need to see the text box border.

6 Double-click the border of the text box   To open the Format Text Box dialog box.

   Click the **Colors and Lines** tab   If necessary.

   Under Line, from the Color list, select **No Line**

   Click **OK**

7 Deselect the text box

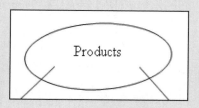

The border of the text box is removed.

8 Remove the borders of the other text boxes

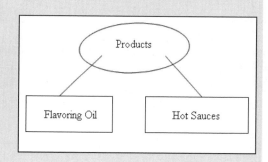

9 Update and close the document

Conceptual diagrams

Explanation

You can use conceptual diagrams to represent data or information. For example, you can use a bar chart to represent the sales for the last five years.

The Diagram Gallery, shown in Exhibit 7-10, helps you create some of the commonly used standard diagrams, such as organizational charts, cycle diagrams, or Venn diagrams. When you insert a diagram from the Diagram Gallery, the corresponding toolbar also appears. You can then use that toolbar for formatting the diagram.

Exhibit 7-10: The Diagram Gallery

To insert a conceptual diagram into a document:

1 Display the Drawing toolbar.
2 Place the insertion point where you want to insert the diagram.
3 Click the Insert Diagram or Organization Chart button.
4 From the Diagram Gallery, select a type.
5 Click OK to insert a diagram within a drawing canvas. The corresponding toolbar appears.
6 Enter the text in the appropriate boxes.
7 Use the Formatting toolbar to modify the diagram. You can add or delete text boxes from the chart.
8 Use the resizing handle to move or change the shape of the selected objects.

Some of the conceptual diagrams that you can create by using the Diagram Gallery are described in the following table:

Diagram	Description
Organization Chart	Shows the hierarchical relationships between elements. For example, use this chart to represent positions in an organization.
Cycle Diagram	Shows the steps of a cyclical process. For example, use this diagram to describe the formation of rain.
Radial Diagram	Shows the relationships of different elements to a core element. For example, use this diagram to show the structure of an atom.
Pyramid Diagram	Shows foundation-based relationships. For example, use this diagram to show different layers of the atmosphere.
Venn Diagram	Shows areas of overlap between elements. For example, if you want to represent the qualification and experience of employees in an organization, the elements that represent the number of post-graduates might overlap with the elements that represent the number of employees with more than two years of experience.
Target Diagram	Shows steps leading toward a goal. For example, use this diagram to show the different steps involved in software development.

Do it!

D-4: Inserting a conceptual diagram

Here's how	Here's why
1 Open Chart	From the current unit folder.
Save the document as **My chart**	In the current unit folder.
2 Go to the end of the document	
3 Click  [icon]	To open the Diagram Gallery dialog box, shown in Exhibit 7-10.
4 Examine the diagram types	When you click a diagram type, its name and a brief description appear in the Diagram Gallery.
5 Select Organization Chart as indicated	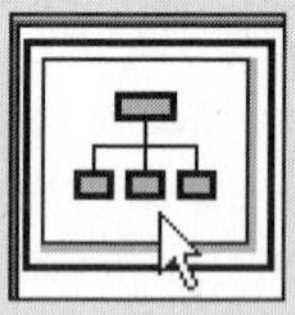 You'll insert this chart into the document.
Click **OK**	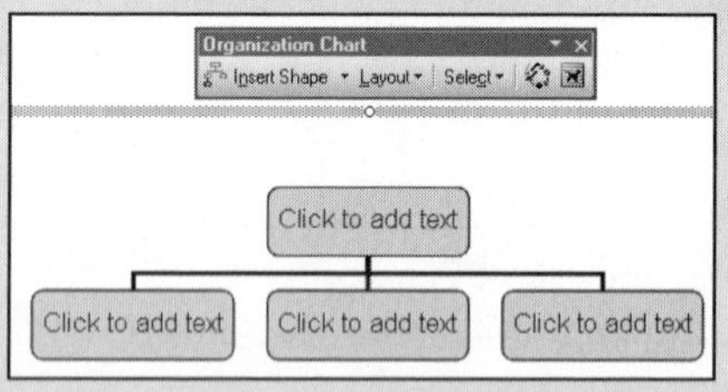 The chart and the Organization Chart toolbar appear.
6 Select the third text box	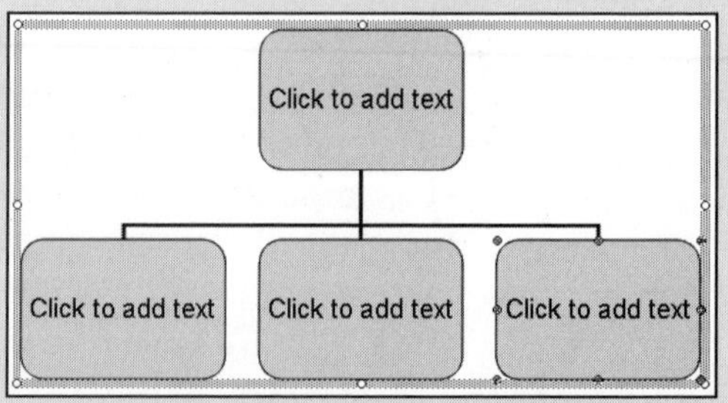 Round selection handles appear when the text box is selected.
Press (DELETE)	To delete the rightmost text box.
7 In the text boxes, enter text as shown	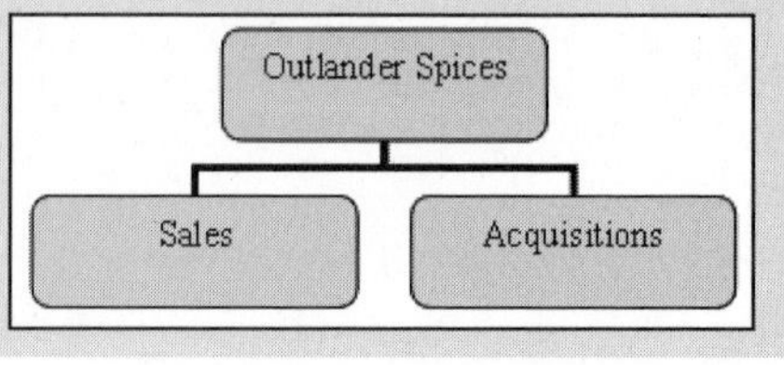

8 Select the Acquisitions box

You'll add two boxes under this text box.

Display the Insert Shape menu, as shown

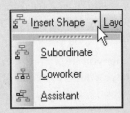

(On the Organization Chart toolbar.) You can add boxes for subordinates, coworkers, and assistants. By default, when you click Insert Shape, a Subordinate box is added.

Choose **Subordinate**

To insert a subordinate box below Acquisitions.

Insert another subordinate box for Acquisitions

Click Insert Shape, and choose Subordinate.

9 In the subordinate boxes, enter **Spices** and **Food**, as shown

10 Insert two subordinate boxes under the Sales box

Enter the text, as shown

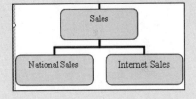

11 Click [icon]

(On the Organization Chart toolbar.) To open the Organization Chart Style Gallery dialog box.

Select **Double Outline**

To see a preview of the selection.

Click **OK**

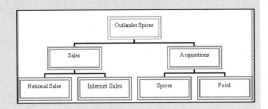

To apply the Double Outline format to the organization chart.

12 Update the document

Callouts

Explanation

A *callout* is text used for labeling pictures or graphics. Unlike text boxes, callouts have a variety of shapes and sizes. You can insert callouts by using the AutoShapes button on the Drawing toolbar.

After you insert a callout, you can resize it by using its sizing handles. You can also move a callout by dragging it. Callouts are visible only in Print Layout and Web Layout views.

To create a callout:

1   Click AutoShapes on the Drawing toolbar.
2   Choose Callouts to display a submenu.
3   Click the type of callout you want to insert.
4   Click where you want to insert the callout.
5   Enter text in the callout.

Do it!

D-5:   Creating a callout

Here's how	Here's why
1 Click **AutoShapes**	Lines ▶ Connectors ▶ Basic Shapes ▶ Block Arrows ▶ Flowchart ▶ Stars and Banners ▶ Callouts ▶ More AutoShapes... (On the Drawing toolbar.) Word offers a wide variety of shapes that can be added to a document.
2 On the menu, choose **Callouts**	Again, Word offers a variety of callouts.
Choose [⌐□]	To add a line callout. The shape of the pointer changes to a crosshair.

3 Start at the right side of the Acquisitions box, and drag up and to the right

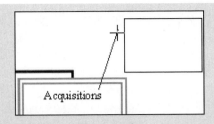

To add a line callout that points to the Acquisitions box.

4 Click within the callout

(If necessary.) To place the insertion point inside the callout.

In the callout, enter your name

5 Deselect the callout

Your name appears in the callout that points to the Acquisitions box.

Deselect the organization chart

6 Update and close the document

Unit summary: Working with graphics and objects

Topic A In this topic, you learned how to insert **graphics** from files into a document. You also inserted pictures by using the Clip Art task pane. In addition, you modified, resized, moved, and wrapped text around the graphics. You also learned how to change the contrast and brightness of graphics.

Topic B In this topic, you learned how to insert **WordArt** into a document. You also inserted **symbols**.

Topic C In this topic, you learned how to apply **background** colors and **fill effects** to a document. You also created a **watermark** for the background of the document. In addition, you learned about **themes** and how they can be used to create a consistent look throughout a document.

Topic D In this topic, you used the Drawing toolbar to draw lines and shapes. You experimented with changing the size of the **drawing canvas**. You also learned how to **group objects** so you can treat them as one. And you created **text boxes** and **callouts**.

Independent practice activity

1 Open Update, and save it as **My update**.

2 At the beginning of the document, insert the clip art image from the Business category, as shown in Exhibit 7-11. Reduce the size of the image to 75%.

3 Format the image to the right of the text "Outlander Spices." (*Hint:* Use the Square wrapping style.)

4 Close the Clip Art task pane.

5 Compare your work with Exhibit 7-11.

6 At the end of the document, insert **Project team** in any WordArt style. (*Hint*: Put the WordArt on a new, blank line at the end of the document.)

7 Under the WordArt, insert the organization chart that's shown in Exhibit 7-12. (Your selected WordArt might differ from the exhibit.)

8 Apply the Beveled Gradient AutoFormat to the new organization chart.

9 Apply the Compass theme to the document.

10 Compare your document to Exhibit 7-12.

11 Close the Organization Chart toolbar and the Drawing toolbar.

12 Update and close the document.

Exhibit 7-11: The document My update after Step 4 of the Independent Practice Activity

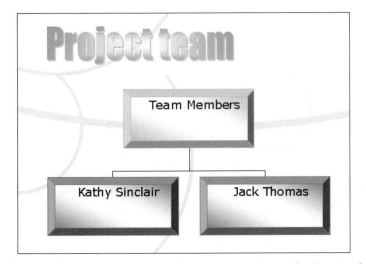

Exhibit 7-12: The WordArt and organization chart after Step 9 of the Independent Practice Activity

Review questions

1 What happens to existing formatting in a document when a theme is applied?

2 What is the difference between a text box and a callout?

3 Which command is used to insert graphics from a file?

   A Insert, Clip Art

   B Insert, Picture, From File

   C Insert, File.

   D Insert, File, From File

4 Name two ways to insert Clip Art into a document.

5 What is the difference between resizing and cropping graphics?

6 Name two methods that can be used to resize a graphic.

7 When moving a graphic by dragging, what should be avoided?

8 Which feature enables you to position document text squarely around a picture?

  A Text wrapping

  B Advanced Layout

  C Watermark

  D Picture Layout

9 Name two ways to split a window.

10 If you are creating a title page with copyright information, how can you add the copyright mark?

11 Which are the four background fill effects?

  A Animated, Texture, Theme, Picture

  B Gradient, Texture, Color, Watermark

  C Gradient, Texture, Pattern, Picture

  D Animated, Color, Pattern, Picture

Unit 8

Document templates

Unit time: 40 minutes

Complete this unit, and you'll know how to:

A Use a template to create a document.

B Create and protect document templates, view and edit document properties, and add and modify template fields.

Topic A: Template basics

This topic covers the following Microsoft Office Specialist exam objective.

#	Objective
WW03S-5-1	Creating new document types using templates

Using a template to create a document

Explanation

Templates help provide a uniform structure for your documents. *Templates* are predesigned documents that contain formatting and, in some cases, often-used text or placeholder text.

Word supplies several built-in templates that you can use to create documents, such as letters, faxes, memos, and résumés. One standard template provided in Word is the Normal template. When you click the New button on the Standard toolbar, Word creates a blank document based on the Normal template. The template settings are automatically applied to anything entered in this new document. However, you can modify this template to change its default settings.

To use a built-in template:

1   Choose File, New to open the New Document task pane.

2   In the task pane, under Templates, click On my computer to open the Templates dialog box. This dialog box has various tabs, such as General, Memos, and Letters & Faxes, which contain corresponding templates.

3   Click the tab containing the template you want to use. For example, if you want to create a memo, click the Memos tab, and select one of the templates shown in Exhibit 8-1.

4   Click OK.

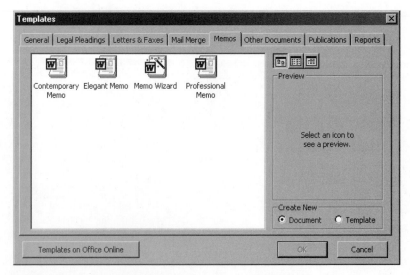

Exhibit 8-1: The Memos tab of the Templates dialog box

Do it!

A-1:   Using a built-in template

Here's how	Here's why
1 Choose **File**, **New...**	To display the New Document task pane on the right of the window.
In the New Document task pane, click **On my computer**	**Templates** Search online for: [ ] [Go] 📇 Templates on Office Online 📝 On my computer... 📄 On my Web sites...
	To open the Templates dialog box. The General tab is activated with the Blank Document template selected by default.
Explore the eight tabs	(In the Templates dialog box.) Word divides the built-in templates into eight categories, represented by the tabs in the Templates dialog box. Each tab contains templates and template wizards suited to that category.
2 Click the **Memos** tab	To see the templates you can use to create memos, as shown in Exhibit 8-1.
3 Select **Professional Memo**	Preview **Memo**
	To create a new document with this template. A sample of the selected template appears in the Preview area.
Click **OK**	**Memo** **To:** [Click **here** and type name] **From:** [Click **here** and type name]
	A new document based on the Professional Memo template opens. Word provides fields that contain prompts for entering the address information.

4 Save the document as **My memo**

In the current unit folder.

5 Click in the To field, as shown

To:	[Click **here** and type name]
From:	[Click **here** and type name]

The gray shading indicates that you've selected a field. A field can be used as a placeholder for the text to be entered.

In the To field, enter **Cedric Stone**

6 In the From field, enter **Ann Salinski**

7 Update and close the document

Template wizards

Explanation

Template wizards provide step-by-step instructions for creating a document from a built-in Word template. For example, the Letter Wizard prompts you to specify the letter format as well as recipient and sender information. You might not need a wizard for simple documents. However, wizards are useful for creating complicated documents, such as résumés or Web pages.

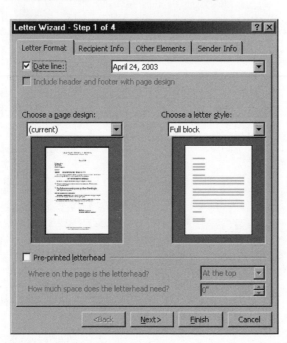

Exhibit 8-2: The Letter Format tab in the Letter Wizard dialog box

Do it!

A-2: Using a template wizard to create a letter

Here's how	Here's why
1 Choose **File**, **New...**	To display the New Document task pane.
Observe the Recently used templates section	

Templates

Search online for:

[_____] [Go]

🖳 Templates on Office Online

📄 On my computer...

📁 On my Web sites...

Recently used templates

Professional Memo

	Word displays the four most recently used templates.
Search for the templates on your computer	In the New Document task pane, click On my computer.
2 Click the **Letters & Faxes** tab	To see the templates you can use to create letters or faxes.
3 Select **Letter Wizard**	

Letter Wizard

4 Click **OK**	

Letter Wizard   ✕

Welcome to the Letter Wizard.

⦿ Send one letter

◯ Send letters to a mailing list

[OK] [Cancel]

	A new document is created, and the Letter Wizard dialog box appears. Send one letter is selected by default.
5 Click **OK**	The Letter Format tab of Step 1 of 4 in the Letter Wizard appears, as shown in Exhibit 8-2. Each dialog box tab is addressed by a separate wizard step.

6 From the Date line list, select the indicated format

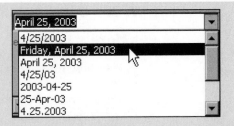

From the Choose a page design list, select **Contemporary Letter**

You'll see the preview in the sample. You'll accept the Full block letter style.

Click **Next**

The Recipient Info tab of the Letter Wizard is activated.

7 In the Recipient's name box, enter **Jack Thomas**

Recipient's name: Jack Thomas

In the Delivery address box, enter the address as shown

Delivery address:
Outlander Spices
100 Main Street
Portland, OR 90001

Under Salutation, select **Business**

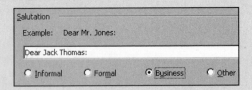

The text next to "Example" changes based on the salutation you choose.

Click **Next**

To move to the Other Elements tab.

8 Check **Reference line**

The options in the list are now available.

From the list, select **Reference:**

You'll insert a reference number for this letter.

After Reference:, enter **A012**

9 Check **Mailing instructions**

The options in the list are now available.

From the list, select **CONFIDENTIAL**

10	Check **Subject**	The options in the list are now available. In the Subject list, "Subject:" appears.
	Edit the Subject list as shown	☑ Subject: [Subject: Recruitment in Midwest]
	Click **Next**	The options on the Sender Info tab appear.
11	Observe the Sender's name	Based on the user profile, your name is entered automatically. You can change the name if you want.
	In the Return address box, enter the address as shown	Return address: Outlander Spices 22 Oak Street Chicago, IL 60601 ☐ Omit
12	From the Complimentary closing list, select **Sincerely,**	If necessary.
	In the Job title box, enter **VP, Financial Services**	To specify the designation.
	In the Company box, enter **Outlander Spices**	To specify the name of the company.
13	Press TAB	Preview Sincerely, Student01 VP, Financial Services Outlander Spices
		All the data entered is visible in the Preview area.
	Click **Finish**	A letter is created with the information you provided.
14	Save the document as **My letter**	
15	Close the document	

Topic B: Creating templates

This topic covers the following Microsoft Office Specialist exam objectives.

#	Objective
WW03S-5-2	Reviewing and modifying the document summary
WW03S-5-2	Reviewing word, paragraph and character counts (e.g., Word Count)
WW03E-2-3	Inserting and modifying fields
WW03E-4-4	Setting formatting restrictions
WW03E-4-4	Applying passwords to documents and forms
WW03E-4-6	Inserting and editing summary and custom information in document properties
WW03E-5-3	Changing the default file location for templates

Saving a document as a template

Explanation

Any document can be saved as a template. Then, you can create other documents based on that template.

To save a document as a template:

1   Open the document that you want to save as a template.
2   Choose File, Save As.
3   From the Save as type list, select Document Template. Word displays the Templates folder.
4   In the File name box, type a name for the template. Word uses the .dot extension for templates.
5   Click Save to save the template.

Storing templates

By default, for a Windows 2000 installation, new templates are stored on your local drive in the Documents and Settings*User_name*\\Application Data\\Microsoft\\Templates folder. (User_name represents the computer user.) Templates stored in this folder appear on the General tab of the Templates dialog box.

If you want your template to be listed on a different tab in the Templates dialog box, you have two options:

- To save your template on an existing tab, create a new folder with the name that matches the desired tab, and save your template file in that new folder.
- To save your template on a new category tab, create a new folder with the desired name, and save your template file in that new folder. Your custom tab will be added to the Templates dialog box.

If you want to share a template with other users, your system administrator can create a shared folder on your network. To gain access to templates in this shared folder, specify the location of this folder in your File Locations settings.

To check or change your File Location settings:

1 Choose Tools, Options to open the Options dialog box.

2 Click the File Locations tab.

3 Verify or modify the User template or Workgroup template locations. You can access the templates in both locations from the Templates dialog box.

4 Click OK to close the Options dialog box.

Do it!

B-1:   Creating a template from a document

Here's how	Here's why
1 Open Note	(From the current unit folder.) You'll create a template based on this document.
2 Choose **File**, **Save As...**	To open the Save As dialog box.
3 From the Save as type list, select **Document Template**	File name: [Note] Save as type: [Document Template]
	To save the document as a template. Word uses the .dot extension for templates.
Edit the File name box to read **My note**	To save the template as My note.dot.
4 Display the Save in list	Save As Save in: [Templates] Desktop My Computer 3½ Floppy (A:) NEW VOLUME (C:) Documents and Settings Student01.OUTLANDERS... Application Data Microsoft [Templates] My Recent Documents Desktop
	The default template path is C:\Documents and Settings*User_name*\Application Data\ Microsoft\Templates. Files stored here will appear on the General tab in the Templates dialog box.
Press (ESC)	To close the Save in list.
5 Click **Save**	To save the template in the default template path.

Protecting templates

You can protect templates stored on a local disk or a shared network drive by assigning passwords to the templates from within the Save As dialog box. Two types of passwords can be assigned:

- The password to open requires users to enter the password before they can open the template or create a document based on that template.
- The password to modify requires users to enter a password if they want to edit the template and update it.

Password guidelines

- Passwords are case sensitive.
- Passwords can contain up to 15 characters.
- Any combination of letters, numerals, spaces, and symbols can be used.
- Mixing up capitalization and numbers creates stronger passwords.
- Be sure to remember the password. Lost passwords cannot be recovered.

Read-only recommended

The Read-only recommended option encourages users to open the template as read-only. If they modify the template and attempt to save it, they must rename the file. This feature is intended to preserve the original template.

To protect a template:

1 Choose File, Save As to open the Save As dialog box.

2 Click Tools and choose Security Options to open the Security dialog box.

3 Check the Read-only recommended box to prevent users from updating this file with the same name.

4 Under File sharing options for this document, in the Password to open box, enter a password. Confirm the password when prompted.

5 Click OK to close the Security dialog box.

6 Enter a file name, and select Document Template from the Save as type list.

7 Click Save to store the protected template in the Templates folder.

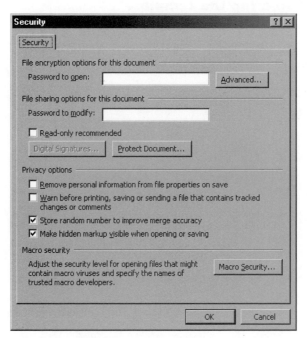

Exhibit 8-3: The Security dialog box

Do it!

B-2: Protecting the template

Here's how	Here's why
1 Verify that My note is open	
2 Open the Save As dialog box	Choose File, Save As.
3 Click **Tools**	

Tools ▾

✕	D̲elete	Del
	Rena̲me	

Add to "My Pl̲aces"
Map N̲etwork Drive…
P̲roperties
S̲ave Options…
Se̲curity Options…
W̲eb Options…
Compress Pictures…
Save V̲ersion…

	The Tools button is in the upper-right corner of the Save As dialog box.
Choose **Security Options…**	To open the Security dialog box, as shown in Exhibit 8-3.
4 In the Password to open box, enter **password**	

Security

Security

File encryption options for this document
Password to o̲pen: ********

	To specify a password for opening the document. You must enter this password if you want to modify or create documents based on this template.
Press (↵ ENTER)	The Confirm Password dialog box appears, prompting you to re-enter the password.
5 In the Reenter password to open box, enter **password**	
Click **OK**	To return to the Save As dialog box.
6 Click **Save**	To save the password-protected template.
7 Close My note.dot	If the template remains open, the password protection won't work.

8 Search for the templates on your computer

Open the New Document task pane, and click On my computer.

Click the **General** tab

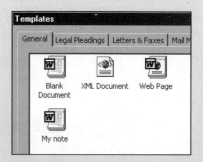

My note has been added to the General tab of the Templates dialog box.

Double-click **My note**

The Password dialog box appears because you've specified password protection for this template.

9 In the box, enter **password**

Click **OK**

To create a document based on the template. This document contains all the text and graphics from the My note template.

Editing document properties

Explanation

You can view the properties of a document by choosing File, Properties. The five tabs in this dialog box provide a variety of information about the document or template. For example, the Summary tab displays the title, subject, and author of the document. Additionally, the template used to create the document is shown near the bottom of the dialog box.

The Statistics tab, shown in Exhibit 8-4, displays a total count of pages, paragraphs, words, lines, and characters with or without spaces.

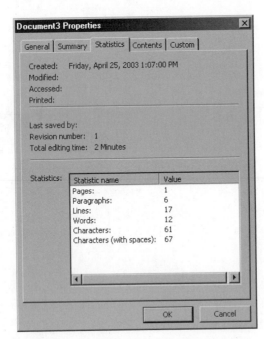

Exhibit 8-4: The Statistics tab in the Properties dialog box

Do it!   **B-3:   Viewing and editing document properties**

Here's how	Here's why
1 Verify that the new document is open	
2 Choose **File**, **Properties**	To open the Properties dialog box for the new document. The Summary tab is activated by default. The Author box displays your name as the creator of this document.
3 In the Company box, enter **Outlander Spices**	To specify Outlander Spices as the company name.
4 Click the **Statistics** tab	

Statistics:	Statistic name	Value
	Pages:	1
	Paragraphs:	6
	Lines:	17
	Words:	12
	Characters:	61
	Characters (with spaces):	67

	To view statistical details such as the number of pages, paragraphs, lines, words, and characters.
Observe the word count	It is 12.
Click **OK**	To close the dialog box and save the changes.
5 In the From box, enter your name	To alter the number of words in the document.
Display the word count	(Choose File, Properties, and select the Statistics tab.) The word count has increased by two, if you entered your first and last name.
Click **OK**	To close the Properties dialog box.
6 Close the document without saving your changes	

Creating custom templates

Explanation

You can create templates that include the text, graphics, tables, and objects of your choice. You can also customize the page layout or page setup settings.

To create a custom template:

1 Click the New Blank Document button on the Standard toolbar to open a new document.

2 Enter the text and apply the formatting that you want the template to contain.

3 Insert any tables, objects, or pictures that you want the template to contain.

4 Choose File, Save As.

5 From the Save as type list, select Document Template to save the document as a template.

6 In the File name box, specify a name for the template.

7 Click Save to save the template.

Do it!

B-4: Creating a custom template

Here's how	Here's why
1 Click	To create a new blank document.
2 Type **Outlander Spices**	The template will contain this text as the heading.
Press (↵ ENTER)	To create a new line.
3 Type **Meeting agenda**	This will be the subheading.
Press (↵ ENTER)	
4 Apply the **Heading 1** style to **Outlander Spices**, and apply the **Heading 2** style to **Meeting agenda**	To format them as a heading and a subheading, respectively.
Center both the headings	Select the text, and click the Center button on the Formatting toolbar.
5 Place the insertion point on a new line below the text	
Insert a table with four columns and four rows	Use the Insert Table button or the Table, Insert, Table command.
Type the column headings as **Date**, **Time duration**, **Issue/topic**, and **Participants**	<table><tr><td colspan="4" align="center">*Meeting agenda*</td></tr><tr><td>Date</td><td>Time duration</td><td>Issue/topic</td><td>Participants</td></tr><tr><td></td><td></td><td></td><td></td></tr><tr><td></td><td></td><td></td><td></td></tr></table>
	To provide a general format that can be used to create agendas.
6 Save this file as a document template named **My agenda**	In the Save As dialog box, select Document Template from the Save as type list. Enter "My agenda" in the File name box. You can save the template in the default template path.

Adding fields to templates

Explanation

Fields are placeholders for data that can change, such as the current date and time. You can insert fields in a template or a document to represent dynamically changing information.

To insert a field in a template:

1 Place the insertion point where you want to insert a field.

2 Choose Insert, Field to open the Field dialog box, shown in Exhibit 8-5.

3 Under Categories, select a category. You can select the Date and Time category to insert fields such as the date when the document was created or last saved.

4 Under Field names, select the appropriate field. A description of the field appears in the Description area.

5 Click OK.

In the document, fields appear with gray shading when they're selected. However, you can change the field shading option to Never or Always. To do so, choose Tools, Options, and use the View tab to select the desired field shading option. Each field has an associated *field code*, which is the underlying formula that gives the necessary result.

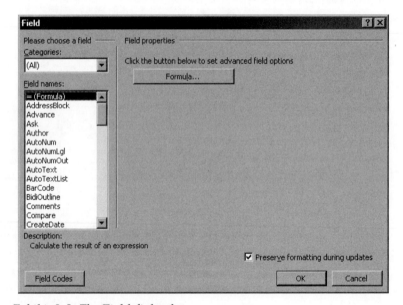

Exhibit 8-5: The Field dialog box

Do it!   ## B-5:   Adding fields to a template

Here's how	Here's why
1 Place the insertion point as shown	**Outlander Spices** *Meeting agenda|*
Press (↵ ENTER)	
2 Type **Created on:**	You'll insert the creation date beside this text.
Press (SPACEBAR)	
3 Choose **Insert**, **Field...**	To open the Field dialog box, as shown in Exhibit 8-5.
4 From the Categories list, select **Date and Time**	**Field** Please choose a field Categories: (All) (All) Date and Time Document Automation Document Information Equations and Formulas Index and Tables Links and References Mail Merge Numbering User Information
	To view the fields available in this category. Each category contains field names that are applicable for that category. The description explains the function of the selected field.
In the Field names list, verify that CreateDate is selected	Field names: CreateDate Date EditTime PrintDate SaveDate Time
	To insert the document creation date.
Click **OK**	Created on: 4/25/2003 10:55:00 AM Date | Time duration
	Word displays the date and time that the document was created.
5 Press (↵ ENTER)	

6 Type **Created by:**	You'll insert the name of the person who created this document.
Press ⌈ *SPACEBAR* ⌉	
7 Open the Field dialog box	Choose Insert, Field.
From the Categories list, select **Document Information**	To view the fields in this category.
In the Field names list, verify that Author is selected	This field will display the author of the document. Word takes this information from the document's Summary Info.
Click **OK**	Your name appears because you created this document.
8 Update the document template	
9 Create a new document based on the My agenda template	To test your new template. The new document contains all the text, formatting, and fields you created.
Close the document without saving it	

Modifying template fields

Explanation

After adding fields to a template, you can modify their attributes. *Attributes* are the properties of a field. For example, by choosing a different Date format, you can specify how dates are displayed.

To modify a field's attributes:

1 Right-click the field and choose Edit Field to open the Field dialog box.
2 In the Field names list, the selected field should be highlighted.
3 In the Field Properties area, select the desired format from the list of formats.
4 Click OK.

Do it!

B-6: Modifying fields in a template

Here's how	Here's why
1 Verify that the template My agenda is open	If necessary, choose File, and use the recently used files list.
Next to Created on, right-click the field	

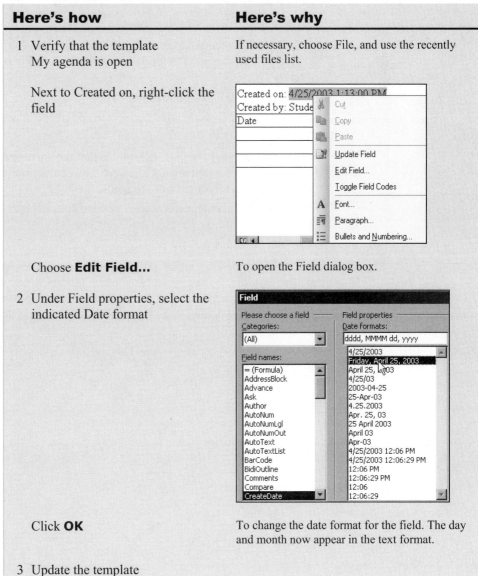

Choose **Edit Field...**	To open the Field dialog box.
2 Under Field properties, select the indicated Date format	
Click **OK**	To change the date format for the field. The day and month now appear in the text format.
3 Update the template	

Formatting restrictions

Explanation

When you create templates, you can apply formatting restrictions to prevent users from changing the formatting in the template. When you apply formatting restrictions, the Formatting toolbar is disabled and only the allowable styles can be used.

To apply formatting restrictions to a template:

1   Open the Protect Document task pane, as shown in Exhibit 8-6.

2   Under Formatting restrictions, check Limit formatting to a selection of styles.

3   Click Settings to open the Formatting Restrictions dialog box. At the top of the dialog box, the option Limit formatting to a selection of styles should be checked.

4   For the Checked styles are currently allowed list, you have the following four options:

   • Click All to allow all listed styles to be applied.

   • Click Recommended Minimum to allow the styles that Microsoft recommends and uses in the Table of Contents and in bulleted and numbered lists.

   • Click None to allow none of the styles.

   • Check the individual styles that you would like to allow in the document.

5   Click OK.

6   A message box might appear, telling you that the document contains direct formatting or styles that are not allowed. You can click Yes to remove the formatting or styles, or click No to ignore them.

7   Under Start enforcement, click the Yes, Start Enforcing Protection button to open the Start enforcing protection dialog box.

8   Enter and confirm a password.

If you want to enable the Formatting toolbar, you need to unprotect the template or document. To do so, display the Protect Document task pane, and click Stop Protection. When the Unprotect Document dialog box appears, enter the password and click OK. You can now modify the document as you wish and then restart the protection.

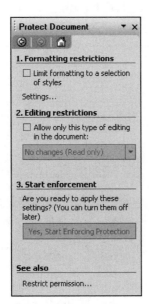

Exhibit 8-6: The Protect Document task pane

Do it!

B-7: Applying formatting restrictions

Here's how	Here's why
1 Choose **Tools**, **Protect Document...**	To open the Protect Document task pane.
Under Formatting restrictions, check **Limit formatting to a selection of styles**	**1. Formatting restrictions** ☑ Limit formatting to a selection of styles Settings...
2 Click **Settings**	**Formatting Restrictions** ☒ Styles ☑ Limit formatting to a selection of styles By restricting formatting to the styles you select, you prevent the ability to modify styles and the ability to apply direct formatting to the document. Select the styles you want to allow to be used in this document. Checked styles are currently allowed: ☑ 1 / 1.1 / 1.1.1 (recommended) ☑ 1 / a / i (recommended) ☑ Article / Section ☑ Balloon Text (recommended) ☑ Block Text (recommended) ☑ Body Text (recommended) ☑ Body Text 2 (recommended) ☑ Body Text 3 (recommended) ☑ Body Text First Indent (recommended) [All] [Recommended Minimum] [None] Formatting ☐ Allow AutoFormat to override formatting restrictions [OK] [Cancel]
	To open the Formatting Restrictions dialog box. The option Limit formatting to a selection of styles should be checked.
Under Checked styles are currently allowed, click **None**	To deselect all styles so that you can select only the styles you need.
Check **Heading 1**, **Heading 2**, and **Table Grid (recommended)**	To allow only these three styles.
Click **OK**	A message box appears, telling you that this document may contain direct formatting or styles that are not allowed and asking if you want to remove them.

3 Click **Yes**

The centered headings are now left aligned.

4 Under Start enforcement, click **Yes, Start Enforcing Protection**

To open the Start enforcing protection dialog box.

In the Enter new password (optional) box, enter **password**

In the Reenter password to confirm box, enter **password**

Click **OK**

To start enforcing the protection. The Formatting toolbar is disabled.

5 Observe the Protect Document task pane

It states that there are no editing restrictions for this document; however, there are formatting restrictions.

6 Update and close My agenda

7 Create a new document based on the template My agenda

The Formatting toolbar is disabled to prevent formatting changes in this document.

Display the Style list

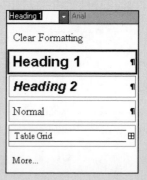

The list displays only those styles that you checked in the Formatting Restrictions dialog box. Users cannot apply other styles. The Normal style is included by default.

8 Close the document without saving it

Unit summary: Document templates

Topic A   In this topic, you learned about **templates**. You used a memo template to create a memo document, and you used a letter wizard template for step-by-step instructions on creating a letter.

Topic B   In this topic, you learned how to create a template from an existing document. You also applied **password protection** for the template. You learned how to view and edit **document properties**, such as the document author and word count statistics. You created a custom template by adding and modifying **fields** and applying formatting restrictions to it.

Independent practice activity

1 Create a document based on the Elegant Fax template. Close the document without saving.

2 Open the document Personal and save it as a template. Name the new template **My employee**.

3 Enter the field labels as shown in Exhibit 8-7.

4 Modify the My employee template to include the following fields:

  • The date when the document was created

  • The name of the document's author

  • The name of the person who last saved the document

5 Update and close the document template.

6 Create a new document based on the template My employee.

7 Save the document as **My info**. If the Saved by field doesn't show your name, select the field and press F9.

8 Enter your name, address, phone number, and e-mail address in the table.

9 Update and close the document.

Outlander Spices	
Employee information	
Created on: 4/25/2003 1:37:00 PM Created by: Student01 Saved by: Student01	
Name	
Address	

Exhibit 8-7: The fields in the My employee template after Step 7 of the Independent Practice Activity

Review questions

1 When you create a new Word document, which template is used by default?

2 What are the steps for creating a new document based on a letter template?

3 How can you make sure that your new template appears on the Memos tab of the Templates dialog box?

4 Which security feature can be used to protect your template from unwanted edits?

A Assigning a password

B Hiding the file name

C Disabling the file sharing option

D Moving the template to a secure server

5 Which tab in the document Properties box displays the total word count?

6 Why would you want to use fields in a document?

7 How are fields identified in a document?

8 Which task pane is used to apply formatting restrictions to a newly created template?

Unit 9

Managing document revisions

Unit time: 50 minutes

Complete this unit, and you'll know how to:

A Track document changes while editing.

B Insert, edit, view, print, and delete comments.

C Create, save, and compare document versions.

Topic A: Tracking changes in a document

This topic covers the following Microsoft Office Specialist exam objectives.

#	Objective
WW03S-4-2	Comparing and merging documents (This objective is also covered in Topic C.)
WW03S-4-4	Locating successive changes in a document
WW03S-4-4	Tracking, accepting and rejecting changes
WW03E-4-1	Setting reviewer's ink colors, setting balloon options, showing and hiding reviewers
WW03E-4-4	Setting editing restrictions

The Track Changes feature

Explanation

While reviewing a document, you can keep track of your edits to easily see all the changes made in the document. You can use the Track Changes feature to view insertions and deletions, as well as changes made by a specific reviewer. A *reviewer* is a person who evaluates a document and changes it.

To use the Track Changes feature, you must first turn it on. To do this, choose Tools, Track Changes, or double-click TRK on the status bar. When you turn on the Track Changes feature, the Reviewing toolbar appears, as shown in Exhibit 9-1.

Exhibit 9-1: The Reviewing toolbar

The Reviewing toolbar contains buttons that can be used to modify the display of the tracked changes. On the toolbar, click the Show button, and choose Options to open the Track Changes dialog box, shown in Exhibit 9-2. In the Markup section of this dialog box, you can specify the marks and colors that will be used to indicate insertions, deletions, formatting changes, and changed lines. These marks are called *revision marks*.

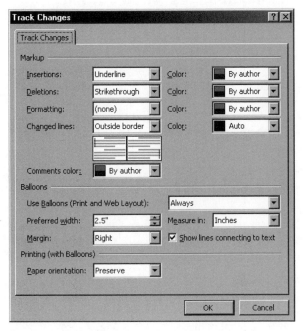

Exhibit 9-2: The Track Changes dialog box

When the document is in Normal view, markups appear directly in the text line. However, you can also view markups in Print Layout and Web Layout views. In these layout views, markups appear in balloons (similar to callouts) in the designated margin, as shown in Exhibit 9-3. Use the Balloons section of the Track Changes dialog box to control the location and appearance of the balloons.

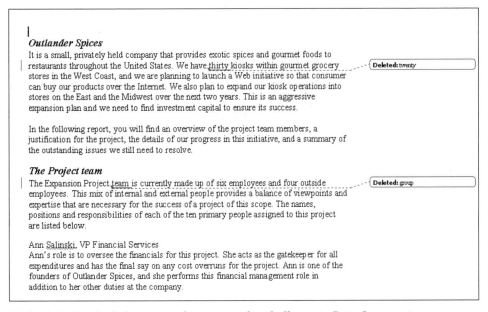

Exhibit 9-3: Tracked changes and corresponding balloons in Print Layout view

Do it!

A-1: Tracking changes while editing

Here's how	Here's why
1 Open Roles	From the current unit folder.
Save the document as **My roles**	In the current unit folder.
2 Choose **Tools**, **Track Changes**	REC **TRK** EXT OVR
	To display the Reviewing toolbar, shown in Exhibit 9-1. In the status bar, the bold TRK letters indicate that Track Changes has been turned on.
3 Click **Show**	(On the Reviewing toolbar.) To display the Show menu, used to control which changes are displayed in the document.
Choose **Options...**	To open the Track Changes dialog box, shown in Exhibit 9-2.
4 Under Markup, display the Insertions options	Markup Insertions: Underline
	By default, inserted text is underlined. However, you can change the insertion indicator to be color only, bold, italic, or double underline.
Press (ESC)	To leave the Insertions setting as Underlined.
Observe the Deletions options	By default, deleted text is indicated with strikethrough marks. You can change this.
5 Change the Insertions Color to **Blue**	Insertions: Underline Color: Blue
	To specify a blue color for inserted text.
Change the Deletions Color to **Red**	To specify a red color for deleted text.
Change the Changed lines Color to **Pink**	To specify that a pink bar appears in the margin wherever a change has been made.
Click **OK**	To save your markup options and close the Track Changes dialog box.

6 In the Project team section, select
   group

> **The Project team**
> The Expansion Project group is curr
> employees. This mix of internal and

7 Type **team**

> | The Expansion Project ~~group~~ team is

The inserted text is blue and underlined. The
deleted text is red and appears with a
strikethrough line. The pink vertical bar in the
margin indicates that this line of text has been
changed.

8 Delete the last paragraph of the
   document

> Kim Leong, Customer Service Representative
> Kim's role is to oversee customer service support to ne
> monitor the demands on our current system and work w
> our telephone system. Kim also will play an integral rol
> of the online ordering system, and he will oversee the c
> documentation for the new system.

The entire paragraph has changed to red and
appears with strikethrough lines.

9 Scroll to the beginning of the
   document

   Change **twenty** to **thirty**

> provides exotic spices and go
> We have ~~twenty~~ thirty kiosks

10 Switch to Print Layout view

The changes appear in balloons in the right
margin, as shown in Exhibit 9-3.

    Switch back to Normal view

11 Update the document

The Reviewing toolbar

Explanation

When someone else edits your work and returns it for your approval, you'll probably want to review their suggested changes. After reviewing the changes, you can either accept or reject them. To accept a change, select the revision mark, and click the Accept Change button on the Reviewing toolbar. You can accept all of the changes at once by choosing Accept All Changes in Document from the Accept Change button.

To reject a change, select the revision mark, and click the Reject Change/Delete Comment button on the Reviewing toolbar. You can reject all the changes at once by clicking the arrow on the Reject Change/Delete Comment and choosing Reject All Changes in Document.

The following table shows some of the buttons on the Reviewing toolbar and describes their functions:

Button	Name	Used to
	Previous	View the previous comment.
	Next	View the next comment.
	Accept Change	Accept the changes in the document.
	Reject Change/Delete Comment	Reject the changes in the document.
	Insert Comment	Insert a comment in the document.
	Track Changes	Turn the Track Changes feature on or off.
	Reviewing Pane	Open the Reviewing pane, which displays the changes you make.

Do it!

A-2:   **Reviewing and accepting revisions**

Here's how	Here's why
1 Place the insertion point at the beginning of the document	You'll review the revision marks.
2 Click ⏩	(The Next button is on the Reviewing toolbar.) To find and select the first change in the document.
3 Click ✎ ▾	(The Accept Change button is on the Reviewing toolbar.) To accept the change.
4 Continue to click Next and accept the other changes in the document	When you have accepted all of the changes, a message box tells you that there are no more tracked changes.
Click **OK**	To close the message box.
Scroll through the document	Because you've accepted all of the changes, the revisions marks have been removed.
5 Update and close the document	

Reviewing changes selectively

Explanation

You might want to view only the insertions or deletions or just the comments inserted in a document. To do so, click the Show button on the Reviewing toolbar, and choose a review type from the menu. For example, if you want to view only the comments, choose Comments and deselect all other options.

You can also view the changes made by a specific person. To do this, click the Show button, and choose Reviewers to display a menu with each reviewer's name, as shown in Exhibit 9-4. In the menu, All Reviewers is checked by default. To view the changes made by a specific person, choose the relevant name from the menu, and deselect all other options.

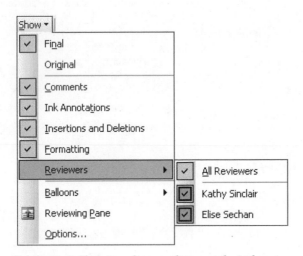

Exhibit 9-4: Showing changes from a selected reviewer

Do it!   ## A-3: Reviewing changes by different reviewers

Here's how	Here's why
1 Open Review	From the current unit folder.
Save the document as **My review**	In the current unit folder.
2 Click **Show**	(On the Reviewing toolbar.) You'll view the changes made by specific reviewers.
Choose **Reviewers**	

> ✓ All Reviewers
> ☑ Kathy Sinclair
> ☑ Elise Sechan
> ☑ Laurie Perry

	By default, All Reviewers is selected. The names of other reviewers who have made changes are listed here.
Choose **All Reviewers**	So that none of the reviewers are selected.
3 Click Show	
Choose **Reviewers, Elise Sechan**	To view only Elise Sechan's changes.
4 Scroll down the document	The last paragraph appears with a strikethrough line because Elise Sechan deleted it.
5 Click **Show**	
Choose **Reviewers, Kathy Sinclair**	So that you can view Kathy Sinclair's changes as well.
Click **Show**	
Choose **Reviewers, Elise Sechan**	To deselect Elise Sechan, and view only Kathy's changes.
6 Scroll up the document	Kathy deleted the paragraph about Aileen MacElvoy.
Close the document	

Restricting edits to tracked changes

Explanation

If you want to protect a document from unwanted edits, you can restrict the edits to only tracked changes. Then, when the document is returned, you can decide whether to accept or reject the changes.

To restrict editing to tracked changes:

1 Choose Tools, Protect Document to open the Protect Document task pane.
2 Under Editing restrictions, check Allow only this type of editing in the document.
3 From the list under Editing restrictions, select Tracked changes.
4 Under Start enforcement, click Yes, Start Enforcing Protection to open the Start enforcing protection dialog box.
5 In the Enter new password (optional) box, enter the password.
6 In the Reenter password to confirm box, enter the same password.
7 Click OK.

If you want to accept or reject the changes in a protected document, you first need to unprotect it. Choose Tools, Unprotect Document, and enter the password. After clicking OK, you'll be able to accept or reject the changes.

Do it!

A-4: Restricting edits to tracked changes

Here's how	Here's why
1 Open Team	From the current unit folder.
Save the document as My team	In the current unit folder.
2 Open the Protect Document task pane	Choose Tools, Protect Document.
3 Under Editing restrictions, check **Allow only this type of editing in the document**	You'll specify the type of editing restrictions.
From the list under Editing restrictions, select **Tracked changes**	No changes (Read only) ▼ Tracked changes Comments Filling in forms No changes (Read only)
	To prevent other users from making untracked changes and from accepting or rejecting tracked changes. You will be the only person who can accept or reject the changes in this document.
4 Under Start enforcement, click **Yes, Start Enforcing Protection**	To open the Start Enforcing Protection dialog box.

5 In the Enter new password (optional) box, enter **password**

   In the Reenter password to confirm box, enter **password**

Anyone who knows this password will be able to accept or reject the tracked changes.

   Click **OK**

To close the Start Enforcing Protection dialog box and apply the password settings. The Protect Document task pane displays a message indicating that the document is password-protected and all edits will be tracked.

6 Under "The project team," change **outside employees** to **external consultants**

> **The Project team**
>
> The Expansion Project team is currently made up of six employees and four ~~outside employees~~ external consultants. This mix of internal and external people provides a balance of viewpoints and expertise that are necessary for the success of a project of this scope. The names, positions and responsibilities of each of the ten primary people assigned to this project are listed below.

In the first sentence of the first paragraph under "The project team."

7 Select **external**

To select the revision mark. The Accept Change and Reject Change/Delete Comment buttons on the Reviewing toolbar are disabled. You're not allowed to accept or reject changes made to the document.

8 Choose **Tools, Unprotect Document**

You need to unprotect the document to accept or reject changes.

   In the Password box, enter **password**

   Click **OK**

The options in the Protect Document task pane appear. The Accept Change and Reject Change/Delete Comment buttons on the Reviewing toolbar are enabled.

9 Display the Accept Change options

> Accept Change
> Accept All Changes Shown
> Accept All Changes in Document

   Choose **Accept All Changes in Document**

To accept all the changes in the document.

10 Close the Protect Document task pane

11 Place the insertion point at the beginning of the document

12 Update the document

The Compare Side by Side command

Explanation

When you're working with different copies of the same document, it's often helpful to compare them side by side. You can do this by using the Window, Compare Side by Side command to view both documents on screen. You must have two or more documents open to use this command.

To view two documents side by side:

1 Open the two documents to be compared.

2 Choose Window, Compare Side by Side [*document name*] to display both documents, as shown in Exhibit 9-5.

3 Click the Synchronous Scrolling button to scroll both document windows together.

4 Click the Close Side by Side button to return to a single window.

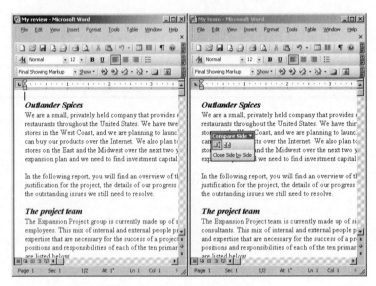

Exhibit 9-5: Comparing documents side by side

Merging revisions by several reviewers

There might be times when several copies of the same document have been circulating for reviewers to mark. Trying to combine all of the reviewers' marks into one document can be a tedious task. To make this consolidation task easier, Word provides the ability to merge all of the document copies into a single document.

Use the following steps to merge the documents:

1 Open the document for which several copies exist. This will be your *baseline* document.

2 Choose Tools, Compare and Merge Documents to open the Compare and Merge Documents dialog box.

3 Select the revised document that you want to merge with the baseline document.

4 Click the arrow next to the Merge button, and choose Merge into current document.

All tracked changes appear as revision marks in the merged document. As in any other document, you can accept or reject these changes.

Do it!

A-5: Merging revisions

Here's how	Here's why
1 Open My review	This document is similar to My team with the exception of two edited paragraphs.
2 Choose **Window**, **Compare Side by Side with My team**	To view both documents in their own windows at the same time, as shown in Exhibit 9-5. You can see that My team and My review are very similar.
Verify that the Synchronous Scrolling button is activated	It is the first button on the Compare Side by Side toolbar, and should appear darker than the other button.
Scroll down to view the revisions	Both document windows scroll simultaneously so you can see the different revision marks.
Click the Close Side by Side button	To return to a single window.
3 Close My review	My team will be the baseline document, and you'll merge the tracked changes from My review into My team.
4 Choose **Tools**, **Compare and Merge Documents...**	To open the Compare and Merge Documents dialog box.
Select **My review**	To select the document to be merged.
5 Display the Merge options	You have three merge options. You can merge the changes of the open document into the selected document. You can merge the selected document into the open document. And finally, you can merge both documents into a new third document.
Choose **Merge into current document**	To merge the changes in My review into My team. The revision marks in both documents appear as tracked changes.
6 Accept all changes in the document	Click the arrow next to the Accept Change button, and choose Accept All Changes in Document.
7 Update and close the document	

Topic B: Working with comments

This topic covers the following Microsoft Office Specialist exam objective.

#	Objective
WW03S-4-3	Inserting, viewing and editing comments

Inserting comments

Explanation

While reviewing a document, you might want to add suggestions or comments. You can view the comment by placing the pointer over the highlighted text. Each comment mark in the document appears with the initials of the person who made the comment.

To insert comments in a document:

1 Select the text where you want to insert a comment. This text will be highlighted after the comment is added.

2 Choose Insert, Comment or click the Insert Comment button on the Reviewing toolbar to open the Reviewing pane at the bottom of the window.

3 Type the comment.

4 Click the Reviewing Pane button on the Reviewing toolbar to close the Reviewing pane, if you like.

5 Point to the highlighted text to view the comment.

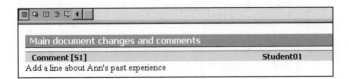

Exhibit 9-6: Adding a comment in the Reviewing pane

Do it!

B-1: Inserting comments

Here's how	Here's why
1 Open Comments	From the current unit folder.
Save the document as **My comments**	In the current unit folder.
2 In Ann Salinski's paragraph, select **Ann's role**	Ann Salinski, VP Financial Services **Ann's role** is to oversee the financials expenditures and has the final say on
3 Click 🔲	(The Insert Comment button is on the Reviewing toolbar.) The Reviewing pane appears at the bottom of the window, and the text "Comment" appears next to your initials. You can enter your comment text on the blank line.
4 In the Reviewing pane, under Comment, type **Add a line about Ann's past experience**	As shown in Exhibit 9-6.
5 Click 🔲	Ann Salinski, VP Financial Services Ann's role [S1]is to oversee the financials expenditures and has the final say on any (The Reviewing Pane button is on the Reviewing toolbar.) To close the Reviewing pane. The text "Ann's role" is now highlighted, and your initials appear next to it.
6 Point to "Ann's role"	positions and responsibilities of ea **Student01, 4/29/2003 1:12:00 PM commented:** Add a line about Ann's past experience Ann's role [S1]is to oversee the fin Along with the comment, Word displays the reviewer's name and the date and time when the comment was entered.
7 To the text "Jack's role," add the comment **Add a line about Jack's past experience**	(Open the Reviewing pane, and type the comment.) In the Reviewing pane, this comment appears below the first one. Comments are numbered sequentially as they are added to the document.
8 Update the document	

Editing comments

Explanation

After inserting comments in a document, you can edit them. To do so:

1 Open the Reviewing pane.

2 Edit the comment text in the Reviewing pane.

3 Close the Reviewing pane.

You can also edit a comment by right-clicking the text to which the comment has been added and choosing Edit Comment.

Do it!

B-2: Editing comments

Here's how	Here's why
1 In the Reviewing pane, add **and qualifications** to both comments	Comment [S1] Add a line about Ann's past experience and qualifications Comment [S2] Add a line about Jack's past experience and qualifications
Close the Reviewing pane	
2 Verify that the comments are modified in the document	
3 Update the document	

Viewing comments

Explanation

In Word, you can view the comments in all views. In Normal view, when you click Next or Previous, the Reviewing pane opens and displays all the comments. The text with the comment is highlighted. You can view the comment by pointing to the highlighted text.

In Print Layout view, you can view the comments within balloons that appear in the margin of the document, as shown in Exhibit 9-7.

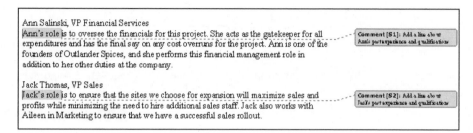

Exhibit 9-7: Comments in Print Layout view

Do it!

B-3:   Viewing comments

Here's how	Here's why
1 Place the insertion point at the beginning of the document	You'll view comments in the document.
2 Click ⏩	(The Next button is on the Reviewing toolbar.) To go to the first comment. The Reviewing pane opens and displays the comments.
View the next comment	(Click the Next button.) The insertion point moves to the next comment.
3 Close the Reviewing pane	
Switch to Print Layout view	The comments appear in balloons in the right margin, as shown in Exhibit 9-7.
4 Update the document	

Printing comments

Explanation
You can print comments along with the comment text and number. To do so:

1 Choose File, Print to open the Print dialog box.
2 From the Print what list, select Document showing markup.
3 Click OK.

Do it!

B-4: Printing comments

Here's how	Here's why
1 Choose **File**, **Print...**	To open the Print dialog box.
2 Verify that in the Print what list, Document showing markup is selected	Document showing markup ▾ Document Document properties Document showing markup List of markup Styles AutoText entries Key assignments You can also print a list of the markups.
3 Click **OK**	To print comments.

Deleting comments

Explanation   You might want to delete some comments from a reviewed document.

To do so:

1 Place the insertion point on the text to which the comment has been added.
2 Click the Reject Change/Delete Comment button on the Reviewing toolbar to delete the comment.

Do it!   ## B-5:   Deleting a comment

Here's how	Here's why
1 Place the insertion point on **Ann's role**	You'll delete the comment for this text.
2 Click [icon] ▾	(On the Reviewing toolbar.) The comment is deleted, and the text "Ann's role" is no longer highlighted.
Switch to Normal view	
3 Update and close the document	

Topic C: Comparing document versions

This topic covers the following Microsoft Office Specialist exam objectives.

#	Objective
WW03S-4-2	Comparing and merging documents (This objective is also covered in Topic A.)
WW03E-4-3	Creating, viewing, deleting versions of documents

Creating different versions

Explanation

Creating different versions of a document enables you to keep the original version intact. The File, Versions command can be used to create a new version of a document.

To create a new version of a document:

1   Choose File, Versions to open the Versions dialog box, as shown in Exhibit 9-8.
2   Click Save Now to open the Save Version dialog box.
3   In the Comments on version box, enter comments.
4   Click OK.

When you create a new version of a document, it is saved with the original file name. So, if you want to open the different versions of the same document at one time, you can do so only through the Versions dialog box.

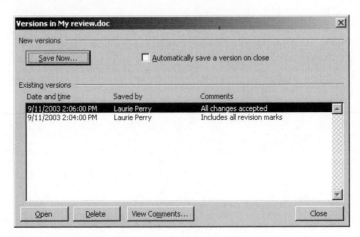

Exhibit 9-8: The Versions dialog box

Do it!

C-1: Creating different versions of a document

Here's how	Here's why
1 Open My review	
Scroll to the end of the document	To view the revision marks.
2 Choose **File**, **Versions...**	To open the Versions in My review dialog box.
3 Click **Save Now**	To open the Save Version dialog box.
In the Comments on version box, enter **Includes all revision marks**	You can identify the versions of a document based on the comments you enter.
Click **OK**	To close the Save Version dialog box and save the new version of the document.
4 Accept all changes in the document	Display the Accept Change menu, and choose Accept All Changes in Document.
5 Choose **File**, **Versions...**	You'll save another version of this document that does not include any revision marks. Under Existing versions, Word displays the details of the document versions, such as the date and time when they were created, the name of the person who saved them, and the comments.
Open the Save Version dialog box	Click the Save Now button.
6 In the Comments on version box, enter **All changes accepted**	
Click **OK**	To save the new version. Your Versions in My review dialog box should resemble Exhibit 9-8.

Saving separate versions

Explanation

When you create different versions of a document with the same name, it might be difficult to distinguish between the saved versions. You can avoid this confusion by saving the new version with a different name. To do this, open the version by using the Versions dialog box, and then save it by using the Save As command. To do so:

1 Choose File, Versions to open the Versions dialog box.

2 Under Existing versions, select the version you want to save with a separate name.

3 Click Open to open the document version.

4 Choose File, Save As to open the Save As dialog box.

5 In the File name box, enter a name for the different version of the document.

6 Click Save to save the version.

Do it!

C-2: Saving a version separately

Here's how	Here's why
1 Open the Versions in My review dialog box	(Choose File, Versions.) Under Existing versions, the most recent version is selected.
2 Click **Open**	[W] My review, 9-11-2003 2-06-00 PM version
	The document version opens in a new window. The title bar of the window displays the document name followed by the date and time when this version was saved.
Maximize the window	
3 Place the insertion point at the end of the document	
Press (↵ ENTER) twice	
Type **Laura Wilkins, Marketing Executive**	To add text to the new version of the document.
4 Choose **File**, **Save As...**	
Edit the File name box to read **My updated roles**	To specify a name for the new version.
5 Click **Save**	To close the Save As dialog box and save the version with a different name.
Close the document	

Comparing versions

Explanation

You might want to compare a version of a document with the original document. When you use the Compare button, a third document is created. In that third document, the tracked changes from the original, or baseline, document are accepted, and the changes from the selected document are shown as tracked. The two documents that you're comparing are not changed. (This feature is not helpful if you want to compare tracked changes from multiple reviewers.)

To compare a version with the original document:

1   Choose Tools, Compare and Merge Documents to open the Compare and Merge Documents dialog box.
2   Check Legal blackline. The Merge button changes to the Compare button.
3   Select the file you want to compare.
4   Click Compare. A third document is created that shows the selected document's changes as tracked changes.

Do it!

C-3:   Comparing versions

Here's how	Here's why
1 Maximize the My review window	
2 Open the Compare and Merge Documents dialog box	(Choose Tools, Compare and Merge Documents.) The Merge button appears in the lower-right corner of the dialog box.
Check **Legal blackline**	The Merge button changes to the Compare button.
Select **My updated roles**	You'll compare this file with My review.
3 Click **Compare**	To open the My updated roles document and compare it with My review in a new document.
Scroll down the document	The only difference between the two documents is that the text "Laura Wilkins, Marketing Executive" is included in My updated roles but not in My review.
4 Close the new document	Don't save changes.
5 Close My review	Word doesn't prompt you to save changes because you have not changed the document.

Unit summary: Managing document revisions

Topic A In this topic, you **tracked changes** in a document while editing it. You also used the Reviewing toolbar to accept or reject changes and to view changes made by specific reviewers. Then, you protected the document for tracked changes by using the **Protect Document** task pane. You merged several revisions by using the Compare and Merge Documents dialog box.

Topic B In this topic, you inserted, modified, viewed, printed, and deleted **comments** in a document by using the Reviewing pane.

Topic C In this topic, you created and saved **document versions** by using the Save Version dialog box. You also compared document versions.

Independent practice activity

1 Open Herbs.

2 Save the document as **My herbs**.

3 Track your changes while editing.

4 Delete the topic **Healing benefits of herbs** on page 2.

5 Accept all the changes in the document. (*Hint:* Click the down arrow on the Accept Change button, and choose Accept All Changes in Document.)

6 For the last line of the document, add the comment **Add a topic on commonly used herbs and spices**.

7 Close the Reviewing pane.

8 Create a new version of the document with the comment **After deleting the topic**.

9 Open the new version. (Maximize the window.)

10 Change the heading "Healing herbs" to **How to use herbs safely**.

11 Accept all the changes in the document.

12 Save the version as **My herbs and spices**.

13 Close the document.

14 Compare My herbs and My herbs and spices. (Maximize the My herbs window before comparing the documents, if necessary.)

15 Save the document as **My spices** and close it.

16 Close the Reviewing toolbar.

17 Close all open documents.

18 Close Word.

Review questions

1 Name two ways to turn on the Track Changes feature.

2 Which toolbar is used to accept and reject changes?

   A Formatting toolbar

   B Markup toolbar

   C Reviewing toolbar

   D Database toolbar

3 How can you see a list of changes that you've made in a document?

4 Why would you use the Show, Reviewers command on the Reviewing toolbar?

5 Which view displays comments within balloons?

   A Print Layout

   B Normal

   C Reviewing

   D Outline

6 Which command is used to create a new version of a document?

   A File, New, Version

   B File, Versions

   C File, Document, Versions

   D File, Send To, Version

7 What happens when you compare a document version with the original document?

Appendix A

Microsoft Office Specialist exam objectives maps

This appendix covers these additional topics:

A Word 2003 Specialist exam objectives with references to corresponding material in Course ILT courseware.

B Word 2003 Expert exam objectives with references to corresponding material in Course ILT courseware.

Topic A: Specialist exam objectives

Explanation

The following table lists all Word 2003 Specialist exam objectives and provides a reference to the location of both the conceptual material and the activities that teach each objective.

Objective	Course level	Conceptual information	Supporting activities
Inserting text, symbols, hidden text and special characters	Basic	Unit 2, Topic C, pp 26-29	C-1, C-2
	Intermediate	Unit 7, Topic B, pp 18-19	B-3
Deleting, cutting, copying, pasting text and using the clipboard	Basic	Unit 3, Topic B, pp 8-12	B-1, B-2, B-3
Checking spelling and grammar	Basic	Unit 7, Topic A, pp 2-7	A-1, A-2, A-3
Checking language usage (e.g., Thesaurus)	Basic	Unit 7, Topic A, pp 8-10	A-4
Creating text for repeated use (e.g., AutoText)	Basic	Unit 2, Topic B, pp 21-22	B-5
Inserting pre-defined text (e.g., AutoText and AutoCorrect)	Basic	Unit 2, Topic B, pp 14-20	B-1, B-2, B-3, B-4
Inserting date and time fields	Basic	Unit 2, Topic C, pp 30-33	C-3
Finding and replacing text	Basic	Unit 3, Topic C, pp 13-17	C-1, C-2
Moving to selected content (e.g., Select Browse Object, Document Map)	Basic	Unit 2, Topic A, pp 8-10	A-4, A-5
	Intermediate	Unit 4, Topic C, pp 20-21	C-2
Inserting, positioning and sizing graphics, text boxes and shapes	Intermediate	Unit 7, Topic A, pp 2-8 Unit 7, Topic D, pp 26-30, 32-33	A-1, A-2, A-3 D-1, D-3
Creating and modifying charts and diagrams	Intermediate	Unit 3, Topic A, pp 6-9 Unit 7, Topic D, pp 34-37	A-3, A-4 D-4
Locating supporting information in local reference materials or on the Internet using the Research tool	Basic	Unit 1, Topic C, pp 16-21	C-1, C-2, C-3
Using the Research tool to select and insert supporting text-based information	Basic	Unit 7, Topic A, pp 8-10	A-4
Inserting new tables	Basic	Unit 5, Topic A, pp 2-4	A-1, A-2
Converting text to tables	Basic	Unit 5, Topic A, pp 5-6	A-3
Applying pre-defined formats to tables (e.g., AutoFormats)	Intermediate	Unit 2, Topic C, pp 16-17	C-1
Modifying table borders and shading	Intermediate	Unit 2, Topic B, pp 13-15	B-1, B-2

Objective	Course level	Conceptual information	Supporting activities
Revising tables (insert and delete rows and columns, modify cell formats)	Basic	Unit 5, Topic C, pp 12-17	C-1, C-2, C-3
Customizing and applying bullets and numbering	Basic	Unit 4, Topic C, pp 32-35	C-3, C-4
Creating outlines	Intermediate	Unit 4, Topic C, pp 18-19	C-1
Inserting and modifying hyperlinks to other documents and Web pages	Basic	Unit 8, Topic B, pp 10-13	B-1, B-2, B-3
Finding and modifying font typeface, style, color and size	Basic	Unit 4, Topic A, pp 2-6	A-1, A-2
Applying styles to and clearing styles from text, tables, and lists	Intermediate	Unit 4, Topic A, pp 2-11 Unit 4, Topic B, p 16	A-1, A-2, A-3, A-4, A-5 B-3
Applying highlights to text	Basic	Unit 4, Topic A, p 9	A-4
Applying text effects	Basic	Unit 4, Topic A, pp 7-8	A-3
Modifying character spacing	Basic	Unit 4, Topic A, pp 7-8	A-3
Applying borders and shading to paragraphs	Basic	Unit 4, Topic C, pp 30-31	C-2
Indenting, spacing and aligning paragraphs	Basic	Unit 4, Topic C, pp 27-29 Unit 4, Topic D, pp 37-40, 42-45	C-1 D-1, D-2, D-4, D-5
Setting, removing and modifying tab stops	Basic	Unit 4, Topic B, pp 20-26	B-1, B-2, B-3, B-4
Applying and formatting columns	Intermediate	Unit 1, Topic B, pp 7-12, 14 Unit 1, Topic C, pp 15-16	B-1, B-2, B-3, B-5 C-1
Inserting and modifying content in document headers and footers	Basic	Unit 6, Topic A, pp 2-6	A-1, A-2, A-3
	Intermediate	Unit 5, Topic A, pp 2-8	A-1, A-2, A-3
Inserting and formatting page numbers	Intermediate	Unit 5, Topic B, pp 9-16	B-1, B-2, B-3, B-4
Inserting and deleting breaks	Basic	Unit 6, Topic C, pp 16-18	C-1, C-2
	Intermediate	Unit 1, Topic A, p 2-4 Unit 1, Topic B, pp 10-11, 13	A-1 B-2, B-4
Modifying page margins, page orientation	Basic	Unit 6, Topic B, pp 7-13	B-1, B-2, B-3
Sending documents for review via e-mail	Basic	Unit 8, Topic C, pp 14-15	C-1

Objective	Course level	Conceptual information	Supporting activities
Sending documents in an e-mail or as an e-mail attachment	Basic	Unit 8, Topic C, pp 14-15	C-1
Comparing and merging documents	Intermediate	Unit 9, Topic A, pp 12-13 Unit 9, Topic C, p 23	A-5 C-3
Inserting, viewing and editing comments	Intermediate	Unit 9, Topic B, pp 14-17, 19	B-1, B-2, B-3, B-5
Locating successive changes in a document	Intermediate	Unit 9, Topic A, pp 6-7	A-2
Tracking, accepting and rejecting changes	Intermediate	Unit 9, Topic A, pp 2-7	A-1, A-2
Creating new document types using templates	Intermediate	Unit 8, Topic A, pp 2-4	A-1
Reviewing and modifying the document summary	Intermediate	Unit 8, Topic B, pp 14-15	B-3
Reviewing word, paragraph and character counts (e.g., Word Count)	Intermediate	Unit 8, Topic B, pp 14-15	B-3
Creating and using folders for document storage	Basic	Unit 1, Topic B, p 12	B-4
Renaming folders	Basic	Unit 1, Topic B, p 15	B-7
Converting documents to different formats for transportability (e.g., .rtf, .txt)	Basic	Unit 1, Topic B, p 12	None
Saving documents as Web pages	Basic	Unit 8, Topic A, pp 4-5	A-2
Printing documents, envelopes, and labels	Intermediate	Unit 6, Topic A, pp 2-5	A-1, A-2
	Basic	Unit 7, Topic B, pp 14-15	B-2
Previewing a document for printing	Basic	Unit 7, Topic B, pp 11-13	B-1
Previewing a Web page for publication	Basic	Unit 8, Topic A, pp 2-3	A-1
Revealing formatting and hidden text	Basic	Unit 1, Topic B, pp 8-9 Unit 4, Topic A, pp 15-17	B-2 A-8

Objective	Course level	Conceptual information	Supporting activities
Viewing reading layout, normal, outline, full screen, zoom views	Basic	Unit 2, Topic A, pp 12-13 Unit 7, Topic B, pp 11-12	A-7 B-1
	Intermediate	Unit 4, Topic C, pp 18-19	C-1
Showing/hiding white space in a document	Basic	Unit 2, Topic A, p 11	A-6
Splitting windows and arrange panes	Intermediate	Unit 7, Topic B, pp 16-17	B-2

Topic B: Expert exam objectives

Explanation

The following table lists all Word 2003 Expert exam objectives and provides a reference to the location of both the conceptual material and the activities that teach each objective.

Objective	Course level	Conceptual information	Supporting activities
Creating and applying custom styles for text, tables and lists	Intermediate	Unit 4, Topic A, pp 2-11	A-1, A-2, A-3, A-4, A-5
Controlling orphans and widows	Basic	Unit 6, Topic B, pp 14-15	B-4
Setting line and page breaks	Basic	Unit 4, Topic D, p 41 Unit 6, Topic C, pp 16-18	D-3 C-1, C-2
Wrapping text with graphics	Intermediate	Unit 7, Topic A, pp 12-13	A-6
Cropping and rotating graphics	Intermediate	Unit 7, Topic A, pp 6-7 Unit 7, Topic D, pp 26-30	None D-1
Controlling image contrast and brightness	Intermediate	Unit 7, Topic A, p 9	A-4
Scaling and resizing graphics	Intermediate	Unit 7, Topic A, pp 6-8	A-3
Inserting and modifying new objects and objects from files	Intermediate	Unit 7, Topic A, pp 2-11 Unit 7, Topic B, pp 14-15	A-1, A-2, A-3, A-4, A-5 B-1
Creating and revising charts using data from other sources (e.g., Excel)	Intermediate	Unit 3, Topic A, pp 2-9	A-1, A-2, A-3, A-4
Sorting content in lists and tables by specific categories	Intermediate	Unit 1, Topic C, pp 17-18	C-2
Using formulas in tables	Intermediate	Unit 3, Topic B, pp 10-15	B-1, B-2, B-3
Modifying table formats by merging and/or splitting table cells	Intermediate	Unit 2, Topic A, pp 5-7	A-2
Modifying text position and direction in a cell	Intermediate	Unit 2, Topic A, pp 8-9	A-3
Modifying table properties	Basic	Unit 5, Topic C, pp 16-18	C-3, C-4
	Intermediate	Unit 2, Topic A, p 10	A-4
Inserting and modifying fields	Intermediate	Unit 8, Topic B, pp 18-21	B-5, B-6
Summarizing relevant content using automated tools (e.g., AutoSummarize)	Advanced	Unit 3, Topic A, pp 14-16	A-7

Objective	Course level	Conceptual information	Supporting activities
Analyzing content readability using automated tools (e.g., Readability Statistics)	Advanced	Unit 3, Topic A, pp 14-16	A-7
Inserting bookmarks	Advanced	Unit 3, Topic D, pp 27-28	D-1
Using automation features for document navigation (e.g., Document Map, Thumbnails)	Intermediate	Unit 4, Topic C, pp 20-22	C-2, C-3
Completing an entire mail merge process for form letters	Advanced	Unit 1, Topic A, pp 2-11 Unit 1, Topic B, pp 12-16	A-1, A-2, A-3 B-1
Completing an entire mail merge process for mailing labels	Advanced	Unit 1, Topic C, p 21-24	C-1, C-2
Adding, deleting, updating and modifying schemas, solutions and settings in the Schema Library	Advanced	Unit 6, Topic A, pp 5-12	A-2, A-3
Adding, deleting, and modifying schemas and transforms to documents	Advanced	Unit 6, Topic A, pp 5-10, 13-17	A-2, A-4, A-5
Managing elements and attributes in XML documents (e.g., adding, changing deleting, cutting, copying)	Advanced	Unit 6, Topic A, pp 5-10	A-2
Defining XML options (e.g., applying schema validation options, applying XML view options)	Advanced	Unit 6, Topic A, pp 11-12	A-3
Creating and modifying forms	Advanced	Unit 2, Topic A, pp 5-8 Unit 2, Topic B, pp 18-21	A-2, A-3 B-1, B-2, B-3
Setting and changing options on form fields and check boxes	Advanced	Unit 2, Topic A, pp 9-17	A-4, A-5, A-6, A-7
Creating watermarks	Intermediate	Unit 7, Topic C, p 24	C-2
Applying themes	Intermediate	Unit 7, Topic C, p 25	C-3
Creating and modifying document background colors and fill effects	Intermediate	Unit 7, Topic C, pp 20-23	C-1
Creating and modifying document indexes, tables of content, figures, and authorities	Advanced	Unit 3, Topic A, pp 7-8, 12-13 Unit 3, Topic C, pp 23-26	A-4, A-6 C-1, C-2
Inserting format and modifying endnotes, footnotes, captions, and cross-references	Advanced	Unit 3, Topic A, pp 9-11 Unit 3, Topic B, pp 17-22 Unit 3, Topic D, pp 30-31	A-5 B-1, B-2, B-3, B-4 D-4
Formatting numbering and marks for footnotes and endnotes	Advanced	Unit 3, Topic B, pp 17-18, 20-21	B-1, B-3

Objective	Course level	Conceptual information	Supporting activities
Creating master documents with three or more subdocuments	Advanced	Unit 3, Topic A, pp 2-3	A-1
Setting reviewer's ink colors, setting balloon options, showing and hiding reviewers	Intermediate	Unit 9, Topic A, pp 2-5, 8-9	A-1, A-3
Setting Web options and saving to a Web server	Basic	Unit 8, Topic A, p 4	None
Inserting and modifying frames	Advanced	Unit 3, Topic E, pp 32-37	E-1, E-2
Creating, viewing, deleting versions of documents	Intermediate	Unit 9, Topic C, pp 20-23	C-1, C-2, C-3
Setting formatting restrictions	Intermediate	Unit 8, Topic B, pp 22-26	B-7
Setting editing restrictions	Intermediate	Unit 9, Topic A, pp 10-11	A-4
Adding users excepted from restrictions (groups and individuals)	Advanced	Unit 2, Topic C, pp 26-28	C-3
Applying passwords to documents and forms	Intermediate	Unit 8, Topic B, pp 10-13	B-2
	Advanced	Unit 2, Topic C, pp 22-24	C-1
Using digital signatures to authenticate documents	Advanced	Unit 2, Topic D, pp 32-33	D-1
Inserting and editing summary and custom information in document properties	Intermediate	Unit 8, Topic B, pp 14-15	B-3
Creating and running macros	Advanced	Unit 4, Topic A, pp 2-5, 7 Unit 4, Topic C, pp 13-15	A-1, A-3 C-1
Editing a macro using the Visual Basic Editor	Advanced	Unit 4, Topic B, p 8	B-1
Creating a custom menu	Advanced	Unit 5, Topic A, pp 2-7	A-1, A-2
Adding and removing buttons from a toolbar	Advanced	Unit 5, Topic B, pp 10-15	B-1, B-2, B-3
Changing the default file location for templates	Intermediate	Unit 8, Topic B, pp 8-9	B-1
Setting default dictionary	Basic	Unit 7, Topic A, p 4	None
Modifying default font settings	Basic	Unit 4, Topic A, pp 5-6	A-2

Course summary

This summary contains information to help you bring the course to a successful conclusion. Using this information, you will be able to:

A Use the summary text to reinforce what you've learned in class.

B Determine the next courses in this series (if any), as well as any other resources that might help you continue to learn about Microsoft Word 2003.

Topic A: Course summary

Use the following summary text to reinforce what you've learned in class.

Unit summaries

Unit 1

In this unit, you used **sections** to format different parts of a document differently. You learned about the different types of **section breaks**, and you inserted them by using the **Insert, Break command**. Next, you learned how to format text into columns by using the **Columns dialog box** and the **Columns button**. You also **inserted a column break** and **changed the spacing between columns**. Then, you learned how to **add a heading across columns**. You also **deleted column breaks** and **removed columns**. Finally, you learned how to **add text** and **headings to columns** and how to **sort text** in columns by using the **Sort Text dialog box**.

Unit 2

In this unit, you learned how to enhance the appearance of a table by **aligning text** in table cells and changing the **text orientation**. You also **merged table cells**, **changed row heights**, and **distributed rows and columns evenly** across a table. Next, you added **borders** and **shading** to tables by using the **Borders and Shading dialog box**. Then, you used the **AutoFormat** feature to format a table. You examined the different types of built-in table formats. You also learned how to **draw a table** by using the **Tables and Borders** toolbar. Finally, you **deleted columns and rows** by using the **Eraser button**.

Unit 3

In this unit, you learned how to **import data** from an Excel worksheet. You also **formatted** and **sorted tabular data**. Then, you learned how to **create** and **modify charts**. Next, you **created formulas** to perform calculations in tables. You used the **Formula dialog box** to **calculate totals in rows and columns**. You also **copied formulas**. Finally, you learned how to **link** and **embed** Excel data in Word.

Unit 4

In this unit, you used **styles** to **format text** in a document. You learned how to **apply** and **create styles**, including **list** and **table** styles. You also learned how to **modify**, **override**, and **delete** styles. Next, you learned how to set up a document **outline** by applying styles. You learned how to view the different document levels in **Outline view**. Finally, you used the **Document Map pane** and **thumbnails** to navigate through large documents.

Unit 5

In this unit, you learned how to create a **first-page header** and **footer** by using the **Header and Footer toolbar**. You also created **odd and even headers** and **footers** as well as **section headers** and **footers**. Next, you inserted page numbers by using the **Insert, Page Numbers command**. Then, you used the Page Number Format dialog box to **suppress numbering on the first page**. Finally, you applied an outline style to a document so you could **include chapter numbers** in the page numbers.

Unit 6

In this unit, you learned how to **print single labels** and **envelopes** by using the Envelopes and Labels dialog box.

Unit 7

In this unit, you **inserted graphics** from **files**. You also **inserted pictures** by using the **Clip Art task pane**. In addition, you **modified**, **resized**, and **moved** the **graphics** and **wrapped text** around them. You also learned how to change the **contrast** and **brightness** of graphics. Next, you inserted **WordArt** and **symbols** into a document. You also added **background colors** and **fill effects** and a **watermark**. In addition, you **applied themes** in a document. Then, you used the **Drawing toolbar** to **draw lines** and **shapes**. You experimented with changing the size of the **drawing canvas**. You also learned how to **group objects**. Finally, you created **text boxes** and **callouts**.

Unit 8

In this unit, you learned about **templates**. You used a **memo template** to create a memo and used a **letter wizard template** to create a letter. Next, you **created a template** from a document. You applied **password protection** to the template. You learned how to view and **edit document properties**. Finally, you created a **custom template** by **adding** and **modifying fields** and **applying formatting restrictions**.

Unit 9

In this unit, you **tracked changes** while editing a document. You used the Reviewing toolbar to **accept** or **reject changes** and to **view changes made by specific reviewers**. Next, you used the **Protect Document** task pane to **allow only tracked changes**. You also **merged several revisions** by using the **Compare and Merge Documents dialog box**. Then, you used the **Reviewing pane** to insert, modify, print, and delete **comments**. You also **created** and **saved document versions** by using the **Save Version dialog box**. Finally, you **compared** document versions.

Topic B: Continued learning after class

It is impossible to learn to use any software effectively in a single day. To get the most out of this class, you should begin working with Microsoft Word 2003 to perform real tasks as soon as possible. Course Technology also offers resources for continued learning.

Next courses in this series

This is the second course in this series. The next courses in this series are:

- *Word 2003: Advanced*
- *Word 2003: VBA Programming*

Other resources

Course Technology has many other books and resources on Microsoft Word 2003 and related topics. You might find some of these other resources useful as you continue to learn about Microsoft Word 2003. For more information, visit www.course.com.

Word 2003:
Intermediate
Quick reference

Button	Shortcut keys	Function
¶	CTRL + SHIFT + 8	Shows or hides nonprinting characters, such as spaces, paragraph marks, and tabs.
		Displays the columns list.
		Splits a cell.
		Distributes columns in a table evenly.
		Opens the Table AutoFormat dialog box.
		Opens the Insert Table dialog box.
		Draws a table.
		Erases lines in a table.
		Opens the Database dialog box.
		Displays the Styles and Formatting task pane.
		Opens the Page Setup dialog box.
		Switches between header and footer.
		Inserts the page number in the header or footer.
		Shifts the insertion point to the previous header or footer area.
		Shifts the insertion point to the next header or footer area.
		Inserts the current date in the header or footer.

Button	Shortcut keys	Function
		Helps you apply the same header or footer or have different headers and footers.
		Opens the Insert Picture dialog box.
		Opens the Format Picture dialog box.
		Opens the Clip Art task pane.
		Opens the WordArt Gallery dialog box.
		Creates an oval.
		Creates a line.
		Creates a rectangle.
		Creates a text box.
		Opens the Diagram Gallery.
		Opens the Organization Chart Style Gallery.
		Opens the Reviewing pane to show the previous comment.
		Opens the Reviewing pane to show the next comment.
		Accepts the changes in the document.
		Rejects the changes in the document.
		Inserts a comment in the document.
	CTRL + SHIFT + E	Turns the Track Changes option on or off.
		Opens or closes the Reviewing pane.

Glossary

Attributes

The properties of a field. For example, by choosing a different Date format, you can specify how dates are displayed.

AutoFormat

A pre-defined table format that contains a collection of formatting options, such as shading, borders, and 3D effects, which you can apply to a table. When you apply an AutoFormat, it overrides any current table formatting.

Ascending

Alphabetical order (A-Z) when sorting

Callout

Text used for labeling pictures or graphics.

Category (X) axis

The horizontal axis, which contains the categories.

Cell reference

Used to specify cells to be included in calculations. The letter represents the column, and the number represents the row. The leftmost cell in a table is known as A1.

Chapter numbers

Including the chapter number or letter when inserting page numbers.

Chart title

The identifying text at the top of the chart.

Column break

A mark that indicates the end of a column.

Comment

A note or suggestion that is attached to selected text. In Normal view, comments are visible in the Reviewing pane at the bottom of the window. In Print Layout view, comments appear as balloons in the document margins.

Cropping

The process of cutting off a portion of a graphic or object.

Datasheet

A series of columns and rows in a spreadsheet whose values are charted.

Descending

Reverse alphabetical order (Z-A) when sorting

Diagram Gallery

A collection of commonly used standard diagrams, such as organizational charts, cycle diagrams, or Venn diagrams that can be inserted in a document.

Document Map

Displays document heading in a navigational pane. This can be helpful when working in long documents.

Drawing canvas

Space where you can work on drawings. The drawing canvas also contains the Drawing Canvas toolbar that provides tools you can use to resize, scale, or rotate drawings.

Embedded data

Worksheet data that is stored in a Word document and does not maintain links to the original file. As a result, any changes made in the original Excel file will not be reflected in the data embedded in the Word document.

Field

Placeholder for data that can change, such as the current date and time. You can insert fields in a template or a document to represent dynamically changing information. In Word documents, formulas are treated as fields.

Field code

The underlying formula that returns the necessary result in each field.

Formula

Used to perform arithmetic operations, such as calculating an average or a sum. You can also copy formulas from one cell to another in a table.

Function

A built-in formula that you can use to perform mathematical calculations. For example, the SUM function adds the numbers in the selected cells. Other functions include MAX, MIN, and AVG.

Grid lines

The lines that help you determine the value of a plotted point.

Grouping

Merging two or more drawing objects into a single unit so you can work with them as a single object.

Legend

The text that explains the values contained in the data series.

Linked data

Worksheet data that is stored in a Word document and maintains a link to the original file. Any change made in the original Excel file will be reflected in the data linked to the Word document.

List style

Defines formats (such as bullets or numbering) for several levels within a list.

Merging cells

Combining two or more cells in the same row or column to form a single cell.

Outline view

Enables you to collapse and expand text to view different levels. You can use Outline view to see how the document is organized and to easily rearrange it.

Return address

The address that appears in the upper-left corner of an envelope. To specify a return address, check Use return address.

Reviewer

A person who evaluates a document and changes it.

Revision marks

The marks and colors that a reviewer uses to indicate insertions, deletions, formatting changes, and changed lines.

Rotate handle

The green circle that appears near the top of a selected object that is used to turn, or rotate, the object on an imaginary axis.

Section

A portion of a document in which you can set certain formatting options, such as line numbering, number of columns, headers or footers, and page orientation. By default, a document has only one section. You can have several sections within a single page and apply different formats to each one.

Splitting cells

Dividing a previously merged cell into multiple rows and columns.

Styles

Named sets of formats that define the appearance of recurring text components, such as headings or captions. By using a style, you can apply several formats in one step.

Symbols

Special characters that include currency symbols, mathematical operators, and arrows. Symbols are inserted in a document by using the Insert, Symbol command.

Templates

Predesigned documents that contain formatting and, in some cases, often-used text or placeholder text. Templates help provide a uniform structure for your documents.

Template wizards

Provide step-by-step instructions for creating a document from a built-in Word template.

Text box

A drawn object in which you can enter text. Text boxes can be placed anywhere in a document.

Theme

A named set of background and foreground images, formats, and styles that is applied to all pages in a document. Themes provide a consistent look among your documents.

Thumbnails

Miniature images of document pages that appear on the left side of the Word window. You can use them to navigate through large documents.

Value (Y) axis

The vertical axis, which contains the data that is charted.

Version

A copy of a document that leaves the original document intact. Different document versions are used for comparison purposes.

Watermarks

Any text or image that can be seen behind the text in a document. For example, an organization's letterhead might have the company logo as a watermark.

WordArt

Text objects with special effects such as shadows, skews, or rotations.

WordArt Gallery

A collection of various WordArt styles that can be used in documents.

Index

Notes

Notes

Notes

Notes